the shirt
off his back

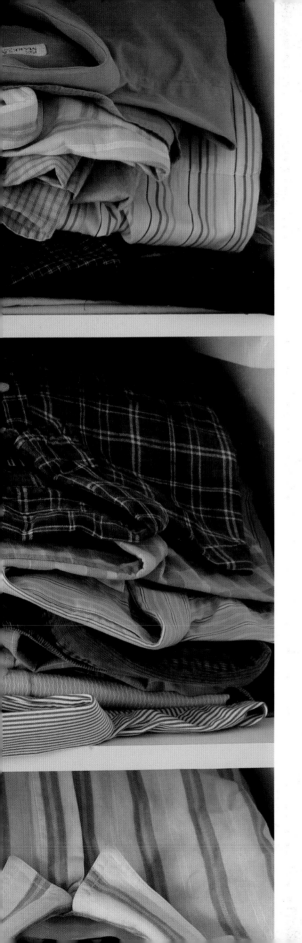

JULIET BAWDEN

the shirt
off his back

30 PROJECTS FOR TRANSFORMING
EVERYDAY SHIRTS INTO A VARIETY
OF HOME ACCESSORIES

photography by
CAROLINE ARBER

BARRON'S

This book is dedicated to Alice π

First edition for North America published in 2011
by Barron's Educational Series, Inc.

First published in 2011 by Jacqui Small llp
An imprint of Aurum Press
7 Greenland Street
London NW1 0ND

All inquiries should be addressed to:
Barron's Educational Series, Inc.
250 Wireless Boulevard
Hauppauge, NY 11788
www.barronseduc.com

ISBN: 978-0-7641-4731-9

Library of Congress Control Number:
2011928835

Publisher: Jacqui Small
Managing Editor: Kerenza Swift
Designer: Maggie Town
Editor: Sian Parkhouse
Production: Peter Colley
Illustrator: Kate Simunek

Printed in China

10 9 8 7 6 5 4 3 2 1

contents

INTRODUCTION

I have always been interested in crafts and particularly
the re-use of textiles. This book combines both passions.

I was taught to sew by my mother, who was a teenager during the austere years of
World War II, when threadbare sheets were cut and resewn sides to middle, and cuffs
were turned to give them a little extra life.

When I was a teenager, I wore a school uniform during the week and I didn't have
the money to buy "going out" clothes for weekends, or at least not as many as I would
have liked. So I, too, recycled. Most weekends saw me adding a new collar to a dress
so it would look different from the last time I wore it.

The idea for this book came about with the first bank crash and start of the credit
crunch in the United Kingdom. Being of a practical nature, I wondered what was going
to happen to all those beautiful shirts that the bankers would no longer need! So I
started making things out of them.

Shirts are one of those items of clothing that seem to age gracefully: the more they
are washed the softer the fabric becomes and the nicer they feel to touch. One of the
first projects I made to utilize that softness was the patchwork duvet cover (see pages
20–23). I love the classic blue-and-white combination, as may be apparent if you look
through the pages of this book.

The range of shirts available are as varied in shape, size, and style as the people who
wear them and, with this in mind, I have created large and small projects, and subtle
and bold ones. Most of the projects are easy and don't require complicated sewing
skills. Some of the smaller-scale projects, such as the booties, are tricky, but not difficult
(see pages 44–47). For items such as the beach bag (see pages 78–81) and the fabric
hamper (see pages 124–127), which use a bigger expanse of cloth, you will need as
large a shirt as possible.

Many of the projects use much smaller scraps of cloth, such as the lamp, (see pages
48–51), the patchwork-covered chair (see pages 56–59) and the retro cushions (see
pages 82–85), so keep all your leftovers to use later.

I have had great fun designing and making the items in this book. I hope that you
will too, and will use this book as a starter for your own creations. Please send them to
me on my blog at *www.creativesalvage.com*.

THE HISTORY OF THE SHIRT

Long ago, when people started wearing clothes, it was the men who were the peacocks and the women, sartorially speaking, the drab peahens.

This is not that surprising, as historically it was men who usually held wealth and power, and what better way to show it off than with their apparel? Until relatively recently, dress was influenced by two main considerations: its adaptation to the convenience and practical needs of the wearer and its function in proclaiming his rank, wealth, and importance.

During the Roman, Greek, and Byzantine periods, the shirt as we know it today was more of a long chemise. By the late gothic period the "chemise" was shorter, but it was still worn as an undergarment. In the Middle Ages, the shirt was a plain un-dyed garment worn next to the skin, and it was only those of lowly origin, such as peasants, who wore shirts or smocks on their own, that were not covered by an outer garment.

In the sixteenth century, men's shirts often had embroidery, frills, or lace at the neck and cuff, and yet the shirt was still considered an item of men's underwear until the twentieth century. According to William L. Brown III in "Some thoughts on Men's shirts in America 1750–1900," even as late as 1879, a visible shirt with nothing over it was considered "improper."

After the formal, utilitarian, and unexciting shirts available during the austere war-time years of the 1940s and into the early 1950s, the 1960s and 1970s brought with them a riot of styles, colors, patterns, and fabrics. The shirt patterns themselves were exaggerated, with curved, almost feminine, fitted shapes, with elongated collars and sleeves that had full, puffed shoulders and grew wide toward the wrist before being gathered up into long hand-covering cuffs. The fabrics, as well, were new to the men's shirt market: silk, satin, and velvet. This new look in shirt design was inspired mainly by the hippy movement and the music scene at the time.

By the 1980s there was change yet again. Ronald Reagan was president in the U.S. and Margaret Thatcher was prime minister in the U.K. Modes of dress, and shirts in particular, are a good social barometer of the age in which we live. The shirt you wear, its color, and the material from which it is made, will place you in a pecking order. If you wanted to get in on the get-ahead society of the 1980s, the style of shirt you wore was important. Bespoke, custom-made shirts made in Jermyn Street in London were, and still are, instantly recognizable because of the fabric—the tightly woven, proper poplin texture. The other signs to look out for are the slight concave curve to the collar bone (cardboard shirts go convex because of the cheap stiffening) and the fine stitching inset $\frac{3}{8}$ in (9 mm) from the collar edge. The key shirt shape for the 1980s gentleman was unshaped with a long tail (for when you send them back to be given a new collar and cuffs).

My husband tells a story of how, as a small boy, he would watch his father dress. His dad would put on a shirt, step into his trousers so they were around his ankles, grab the shirttails between his thighs so the shirt would not ride up, and then pull up the trousers. No shirttails coming out of trousers in those days—a gentleman was always smartly attired!

In the twenty-first century, with world communication being so much easier, a plethora of Internet sites, and shopping channels and so on, choice is vast. The range and fashions of what we choose to wear make us stand out more for our style than our social class. Yet with the current global recession and civil unrest, perhaps this is about to change once again!

DECONSTRUCTING THE SHIRT

When a shirt is taken apart it is surprising just how many elements there are and how much material there is. I have used different parts of the shirt for different projects in this book, and I am sure there are many other ideas that could come from the shirt's shape.

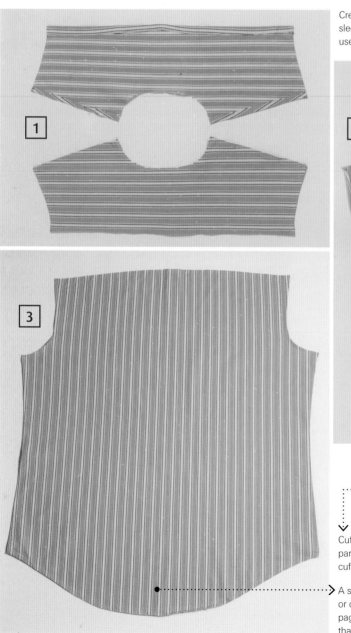

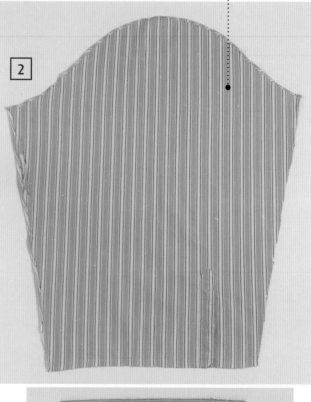

Create a shirt, for either a teddy bear or a rabbit toy, from an upside down sleeve with its cuff still attached (see pages 24–25). A sleeve was also used to make the cord peg bag (see pages 96–99).

Cuffs, forming interesting oblongs, complete with button holes, became part of the upholstered patchwork chair (see pages 56–59). Two other cuffs were used to make wings for the owl doorstop (see pages 92–95).

A shirt back is a very large area of cloth. This can be used for large projects or cut on the cross to make bias strip for binding. The laundry bin (see pages 124–127) and the garden tidy (see pages 100–103) are projects that need large areas of cloth, so look for extra-large shirts for these.

Pockets can be cut off a shirt and then sewn back in a different place such as in our beach bag (see pages 78–81), or they might even be used to create new pockets, as in the garden organizer. I used some of my pockets to make herbal sachets (see pages 60–63).

The tips of collars created feathers and feet for the owl doorstop (see pages 92–95).

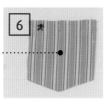

Buttons can be used for their original purpose as a fastening, or as a trim, as on the herb sachets (see pages 60–63), or as eyes for a toy.

A complete shirt or three, including back yokes (1) and fronts (8), can be used to make a headboard cover (see pages 132–135) or, with arms and back cut away, an apron (see pages 52–55).

The plackets of shirts, with their perfectly straight edging, may be used to trim towels (see pages 18–19) or laid side by side to create an elegant book cover (see pages 30–33). They can be wound around the pole of a standard lamp (see pages 48–51), or used to make the mast of an appliquéd yacht (see pages 114–117). The placket from a bright yellow plaid shirt was turned into hanging loops on a garden organizer (see pages 100–103).

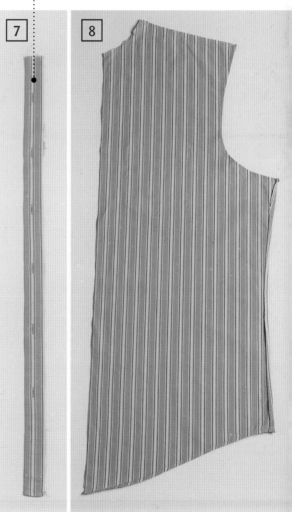

BUSINESSMEN'S SHIRTS

Although it was the striped shirts beloved by workers in the City of London, particularly the bankers, that inspired me to write this book, it is the white shirt that is the ultimate symbol of formality. There is little to rival a pristine white shirt set against a dark suit for distinguished masculine presentation.

Modern shirts first emerged in the Edwardian era and were originally white. Gradually colors were introduced, including the current most popular color—blue.

In past times, when what you wore was prescribed by society rules, a gentleman divided his wardrobe into town and country shirts. Town shirts were made from woven striped fabric in one of the following colors, always on a white background: dark red, mid or dark blue, or gray. It was in 1870 when stripes first entered the gentleman's wardrobe. Known as regatta stripes, they were deemed unsuitable for business wear, as they were suspected of being worn in order to disguise dirt. The pinstripe, popularized by the cinema, particularly when worn with red suspenders, is now synonymous with finance—be it that of the banker or the gangster.

Quality shirts for business wear are made from lightweight, finely woven cotton. The better quality ones are made from the long-fibered Egyptian cotton that has a fine satin texture. A "dress shirt" is a business shirt—a button-front or a button-up shirt. A more formal evening shirt is often worn with a white or black tie.

I have used a mixture of businessmen's shirts to make these projects. The patchwork duvet cover and the striped pillowcase (see pages 20–23) both use my favorite classic combination of white-and-blue stripes. The dining chair cover (see pages 34–37) uses a combination of business shirts in both stripes and checks, with the addition of vintage white cuffs I picked up at a flea market in Amsterdam.

The blue towels, with their boutique hotel vibe, use the plackets of business shirts as a form of simple decoration (see pages 18–19). The book cover uses a combination of shirt plackets (see pages 30–33). This project could be made more masculine by using darker businessmen's stripes. When I saw the formal evening shirt, with its strikingly ornate buttons and small pin tucks, I knew immediately it would make an excellent feminine jewelry roll (see pages 38–41).

SLEEP WELL BED PILLOW

What a good, and potentially amusing, way to re-love an old shirt. As you can see, we made this pillow cover a little tight, so it seems as if it is stretching over a rather pleased-with-itself belly. If you don't want to use it as a pillow cover, then it will work equally well as a pajama or nightshirt case.

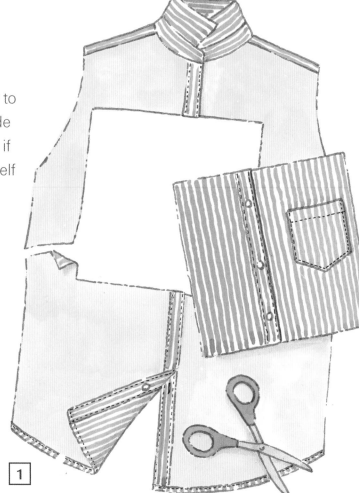

1

MATERIALS

- A shirt with a button-down front
- Matching thread
- A scrap of fabric from another shirt
- Pillow pad

EQUIPMENT

- Tape measure
- Tailors' chalk
- Dressmaking scissors
- Pins
- Needle
- Pinking shears
- Sewing machine

INSTRUCTIONS

1 Measure the pillow. Turn the shirt inside out and lay it flat with the buttons and placket on the top. Measure and mark a square on the shirt with tailors' chalk, the same size as the pillow cushion plus ½ in (1 cm) seam allowance all the way around. If there is a pocket on the shirt, include it. If you want the shirt cover to be tight then omit the seam allowance. Cut away the extra fabric. Cut a second piece of the same size from the back of the shirt.

2 Undo the buttons and then place the shirt front, overlapping as if it were buttoned, on top of the shirt back, right sides together. Pin, baste, and machine stitch all the way around using the ½ in (1 cm) seam allowance.

2

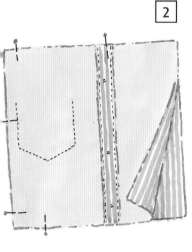

3 Turn the cover the right side out through the button opening, insert the cushion, and fasten the buttons. From a contrasting scrap of shirt, using pinking shears, cut a square of fabric. Tuck this into the pocket as a finishing touch.

3

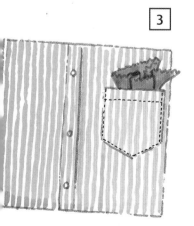

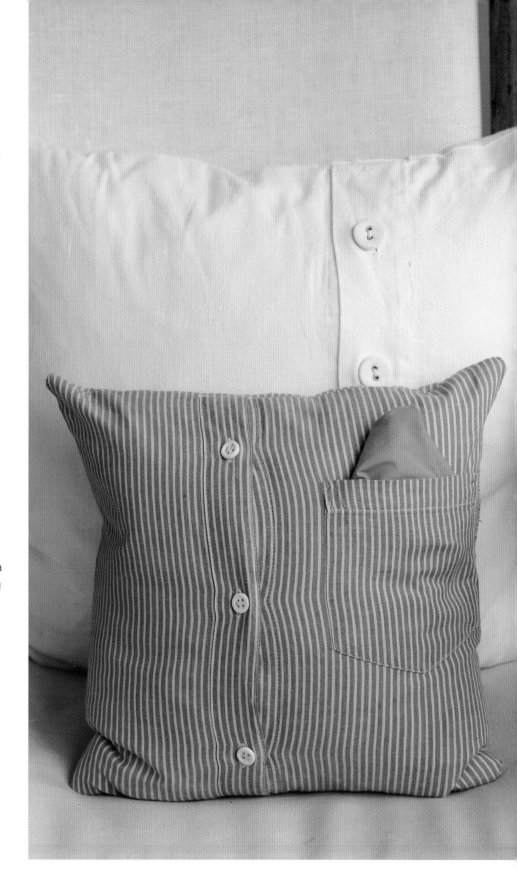

PLACKET-TRIMMED TOWELS

This has to be the easiest and yet one of the most stylish projects in this book. Choose the shirt plackets to either complement the towel colors you have, or add a crazy contrasting color. This is an original gift idea for someone moving into a new home. Buy an inexpensive towel, cut off the label, and then embellish with shirt plackets.

MATERIALS

- A selection of shirts
- Hand towels with woven stripes
- Matching thread

EQUIPMENT

- Dressmaking scissors
- Pins
- Needle
- Sewing machine

INSTRUCTIONS

1 Cut the shirt placket away from the shirt. Trim the placket so it is as long as the width of the towel plus ¾ in (2 cm) seam allowance on both ends (see pic. 1).

2 Turn under the seam allowance on the short ends, and pin the placket to the towel so it covers the flat woven stripe. Baste the placket onto the towel. Machine stitch the placket in place, following the existing stitching lines on the placket (see pic. 2).

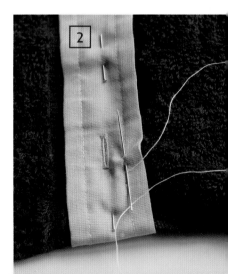

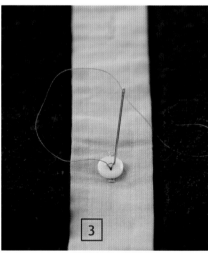

3 As an extra decorative feature, sew shirt buttons over the button holes (see pic. 3). Repeat these steps for each hand towel you wish to decorate.

DUVET COVER AND PILLOWCASE

This quilt is slightly quirky in that the patches are not all exactly the same size. This way, several bits and pieces of shirts can be used up. In contrast, the pillowcase is made from symmetrical strips of shirt, but by using the same colors as in the bed cover, the design is pulled together. For instructions on how to make the shirt for the teddy bears, see pages 24–25.

MATERIALS

- 7 shirts in complementary colors and patterns
- An old sheet or sheeting fabric 53 x 79 in (135 x 200 cm)
- Matching thread
- 6 press studs

EQUIPMENT

- Dressmaking scissors
- Pins
- Sewing machine
- Needle
- Iron and ironing board

INSTRUCTIONS

To make the pillowcase, machine stitch strips of shirt to one another and use a shirt front for the back of the case. Follow the instructions as for the Sleep Well Bed Pillow (see pages 16–17), taking your measurements from your pillow.

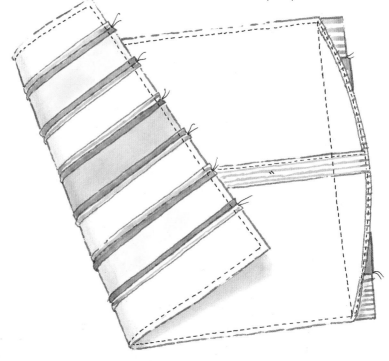

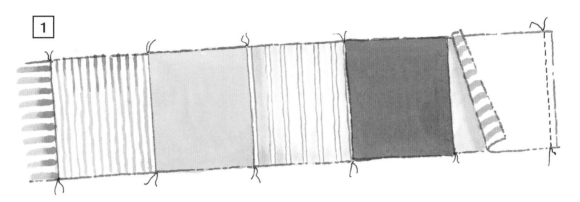

TO MAKE THE DUVET COVER

1 Cut out 231 squares approximately
5 x 5 in (13 x 13 cm) from your shirts.
Using a ½ in (1 cm) seam allowance,
with right sides together, pin and then
machine stitch one patch onto the next to
make rows. Press all seams flat.

> **TIP**
>
> Make sure to place different patterns and
> colors next to one another, and to vary the
> direction of any stripes you use, both when
> sewing the squares together to make the rows
> and when sewing the rows together.

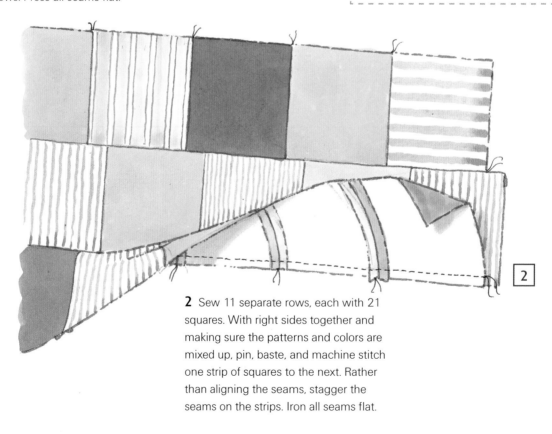

2 Sew 11 separate rows, each with 21
squares. With right sides together and
making sure the patterns and colors are
mixed up, pin, baste, and machine stitch
one strip of squares to the next. Rather
than aligning the seams, stagger the
seams on the strips. Iron all seams flat.

3 With right sides facing in, pin the patchwork onto the sheeting. Trim off the patches that stick out so the sides are straight. Baste and then machine stitch around the two long sides and one of the short sides. Turn the remaining short edge under by ¾ in (2 cm) twice and machine stitch to neaten. Turn right sides out then sew the press studs, evenly spaced, to the inside of both open edges.

3

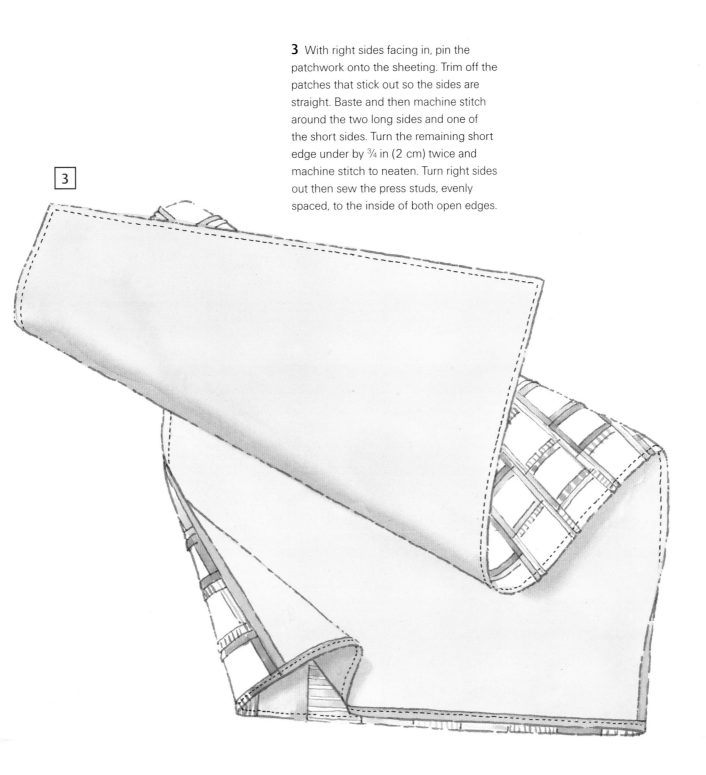

BEDTIME SHIRT FOR TEDDY

This is such a cute look for a teddy, and it is an easy project that you can make with a child. A shirt with a smaller cuff is probably better for a smaller bear.

MATERIALS

- A striped business shirt
- Matching thread
- A teddy

EQUIPMENT

- Tape measure
- Dressmaking scissors
- Pins
- Sewing machine
- Pinking shears
- Needle

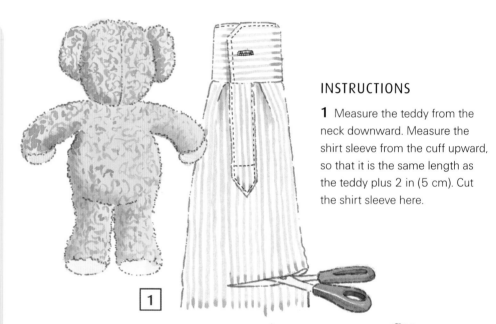

INSTRUCTIONS

1 Measure the teddy from the neck downward. Measure the shirt sleeve from the cuff upward, so that it is the same length as the teddy plus 2 in (5 cm). Cut the shirt sleeve here.

2 Position the shirt sleeve with the bottom of the cuff lining up with the bear's neck and pin the shirt fabric on both sides to indicate where the teddy's arms will poke through. Cut 2 holes where you have measured. Put the sleeve over the teddy's head and pull the arms through the holes. You may have to remove the shirt and adjust the holes if they are too tight.

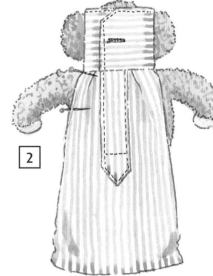

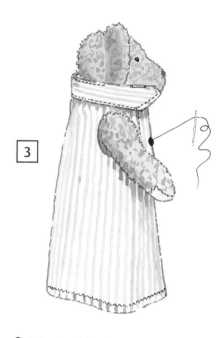

3 Take the shirt off the bear and neaten the arm holes and the bottom of the nightshirt. Turn under by ½ in (1 cm) twice and finish with a zigzag stitch on your sewing machine. Alternatively, use pinking shears to finish the bottom edge. Put the nightshirt back on teddy and fasten the buttons on the sleeve. If there aren't any, you can take some from the front of the shirt and sew these on. For sartorial elegance, turn down what was once a shirt cuff, and is now a teddy's collar, securing it with a few stitches to keep it in place.

PINSTRIPE BUNTING

This is another project that only needs fragments of fabric. Use the brightest striped shirts and cut the flags both vertically and horizontally across the design. This bunting is double sided so it has a more professional finish than that made with only one piece of fabric. Bunting is a spontaneous, easy way of creating a sense of occasion: it can be hung inside or out for holidays, birthdays, or other celebrations.

MATERIALS

- Lots of striped shirts in different colors
- Matching thread
- Colored piping cord or string for hanging
- Paper to make a pattern

EQUIPMENT

- Pencil and ruler
- Paper-cutting scissors
- Pins
- Dressmaking scissors
- Needle
- Sewing machine
- Iron and ironing board

INSTRUCTIONS

1 Make a paper pattern by cutting a pendant-shaped triangle with 2 long sides of 10½ in (27 cm) and 1 short side of 8 in (20 cm). Pin the pattern to the shirt and cut out a triangle of fabric (see pic. 1). Repeat this for twice as many finished pendants as you want.

2 With right sides together, using a ¼ in (6 mm) allowance, pin, baste, and machine stitch two different striped triangles together along the short side. Turn in ¼ in (6 mm) seam allowance along the long edges of the triangles and then press flat (see pic. 2).

3 Fold along the joined seam, then pin and baste the front to the back of the pendant, wrong sides together. Top stitch from the pointed end up to within ¾ in (2 cm) of the top of the pendant along both long sides of the pendant. Make all the other pendants in the same way. Arrange in a pleasing manner, then thread them onto the cord through their open tops, and hang up (see pic. 3).

BOOK COVER

I love it when something such as a shirt placket has an obvious use, as it does here. If it were simply strips of fabric joined together, it wouldn't have the same finish. This project is dear to my heart as it is simple to do and, depending on color choices, can look sophisticated, homespun, or simply stunning.

MATERIALS

- A selection of shirts (the number will depend on the size of the book)
- A shirt for the lining fabric
- Matching thread
- Fusible webbing
- A book

EQUIPMENT

- Tape measure
- Dressmaking scissors
- Iron and ironing board
- Sewing machine
- Needle

INSTRUCTIONS

1 Open the book you want to cover and lay it flat. Measure the width of the opened book, plus an extra 4 in (10 cm) for the wraparound x the height of the book. Cut the piece of fusible webbing to this measurement, and also a piece of shirting for the lining fabric (see pic. 1).

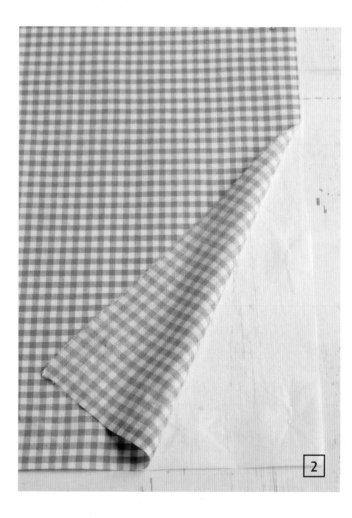

2 Place the fusible webbing on the lining and then, using a hot iron, go over the paper side until the glue has melted. You will see this through the paper. Peel off the paper (see pic. 2).

TIP
In case you end up with fusible webbing on the bottom of the iron, keep some nail varnish remover and a soft cloth on hand, as this will remove the glue.

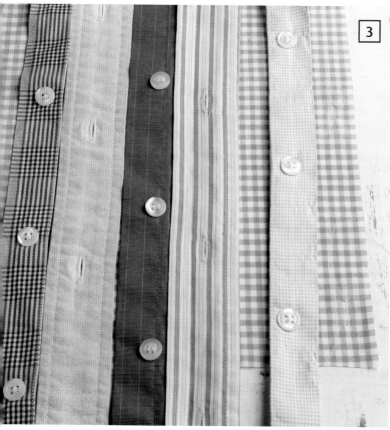

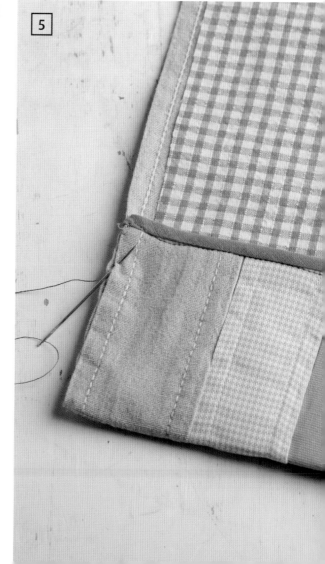

5 Wrap the cover around the book. To make a slip pocket to hold the cover on the book, slip stitch the overlap top and bottom on each side (see pic. 5).

3 Carefully cut the plackets away from the shirts and then arrange them on top of the glue side of the lining, until you are happy with the composition (see pic. 3). Using a hot iron, press the top of the plackets until they stick. Trim the overhanging edges of the plackets so they align with the edge of the lining. If you wish, you can machine stitch each placket into place.

4 To neaten the inside edges of the book cover, turn under by ¼ in (6 mm) and machine stitch. Alternatively, you can finish the edge with a strip of binding cut from one of your shirts.

A CHAIR WITH A DIFFERENCE

This cover gives a chair a real "wow" factor, and the buttoned shirt front makes it easy to slip on and off. Before you make it you will need to do lots of measuring and make a paper pattern. This type of cover works best on an upright chair without any curves or carvings. You will need large shirts for this project. I was very lucky to find one that had a strange false shirt tail in a smaller check in the same color scheme. I didn't have a patterned shirt with white cuffs, so I took some from a plain white shirt and replaced the patterned ones.

MATERIALS

- At least 3 large shirts
- White cuffs (optional)
- Matching thread
- Paper to make patterns

EQUIPMENT

- Tape measure
- Long ruler
- Pencil
- Paper-cutting scissors
- Pins
- Dressmaking scissors
- Needle
- Sewing machine
- Iron and ironing board

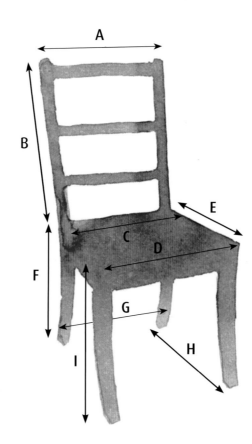

MAKING THE PAPER PATTERN

1 For the front of the chair back, measure A, B, and C, and add a seam allowance of ¾ in (2 cm) to each side and the top—this unusual allowance takes into account the thickness of the chair back, so adjust yours according to your chair; add a ½ in (1 cm) seam allowance to the bottom edge; cut a piece of paper to this measurement.

2 Measure widths C and D and length E, add a ½ in (1 cm) seam allowance to each side and cut out the seat pattern.

3 Measure the back of the chair (B plus F by A and G), add a ½ in (1 cm) seam allowance and then cut a piece of paper to this size.

4 For the sides, measure lengths E and H and heights F and I; add a ½ in (1 cm) seam allowance and cut 2 pieces of paper.

5 For the front of the chair measure height I and width D, add a ½ in (1 cm) seam allowance and cut 1 piece of paper.

INSTRUCTIONS

1 Pin the front and back paper pattern pieces together and slip them over the chair. If the measurement is tight, add some more to your pattern; if it is too loose, move the pins in so that it fits and mark the new seam allowance. Remember, you need to be able to lift the cover on and off (although the back of the finished chair cover will have a buttoned shirt front as an opening). Pin the seat, front, and sides to the pattern pieces already on the chair. Mark each of the pattern pieces—back, front of backrest, seat, front, and sides—so you know where they all go.

2 When you are happy with the fit of the pattern, carefully unpin the pieces and remove them from the chair. Choose your shirts carefully and pin the paper pattern onto the pieces of shirt. You may have to join some pieces of fabric together, as I have here, to get large enough pieces to work with. Remember to use a buttoned shirt front for the back of the chair and center the opening on your pattern piece. Cut out the pieces with dressmaking scissors.

3 Cut the arms off a shirt. If you wish, replace the patterned cuffs with plain white ones from another shirt, machine stitching them onto the bottom of the sleeves with right sides together and a ½ in (1 cm) seam allowance. Fold the cuffs down and press the seams.

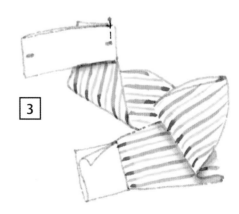

4 With right sides facing in, pin all the fabric pieces together, just as they were on your paper pattern, but this time pin the top of the arms between the back and front of the chair cover, one on each side, 5½ in (14 cm) from the top. I aligned mine with the seam joining two pieces of fabric together. Make sure the arms are enclosed between the front and back pieces so that they will be on the outside of the finished chair cover when it is turned right side out.

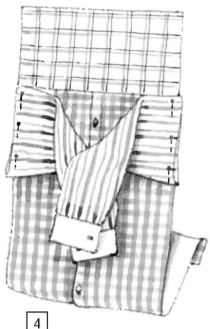

4

TIP
You may find it easiest to pin the back pieces together while the fabric is on the chair, so that you can adjust the pins as necessary to get the seams correct on the chair back.

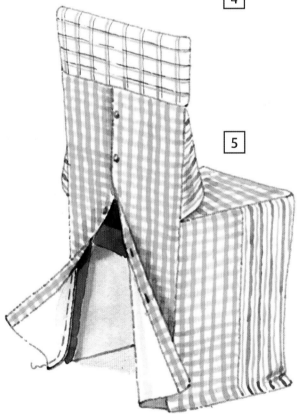

5

5 Baste everything in place. Then turn the cover right side out and slip it over the chair and button up the back to check that it fits properly. Make any adjustments you need at this stage. When you are happy with the fit, machine stitch along the basting on each seam. Then sew a second line of stitching to reinforce the seams. Press the seams and overlock the raw edges. Finally, fold and press the bottom of the shirt ¼ in (6 mm) to the wrong side, then fold over and press another ¼ in (6 mm) and machine stitch the hem.

JEWELRY ROLL

Jewelry rolls are a very useful way of taking both your glittery and valuable items on vacation. This roll has been created from a classic white evening shirt, with a contrasting shirt in pale blue. The pleats are very pretty and the buttons decorative. It is so nice it can even be used at home for storing jewelry, and it's also machine washable.

MATERIALS

- An evening shirt with a decorative pleated front
- A shirt in a contrasting color
- Matching thread
- Paper to make patterns
- 12 in (30 cm) wadding
- Small amount of kapok or cotton wool
- Press stud

EQUIPMENT

- Ruler or tape measure
- Pencil
- Paper-cutting scissors
- Pins
- Dressmaking scissors
- Needle
- Sewing machine
- Iron and ironing board

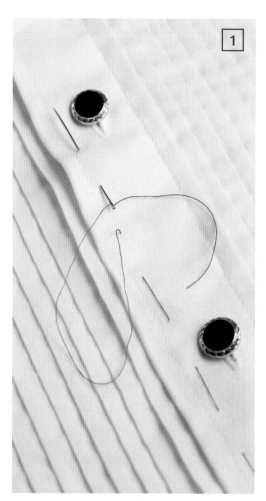

INSTRUCTIONS

1 For the body of the jewelry roll, cut a paper pattern 8 x 11½ in (20 x 29 cm). For the pockets, cut one pattern 6½ x 3½ in (16 x 9 cm) and another 4½ x 3 in (11 x 8 cm). For the ring holder make a pattern 7 x 2 in (18 x 5 cm). Using the pattern as a guide, cut out a body piece from the shirt front (with the placket running down the center, buttons fastened), another from the back of the shirt, and a piece of wadding. Pin, baste, and machine stitch along the front opening of the shirt (see pic. 1).

2 From the contrasting shirt use the patterns to cut the pockets. Turn under the raw edges by ¼ in (6 mm) twice and press flat. Machine stitch along one long side on each pocket to finish the open edge. Pin, baste, and machine stitch the pockets on the other 3 sides onto the right side of the fabric you cut out for the back piece. Divide the bigger pocket in two by sewing a line up the center.

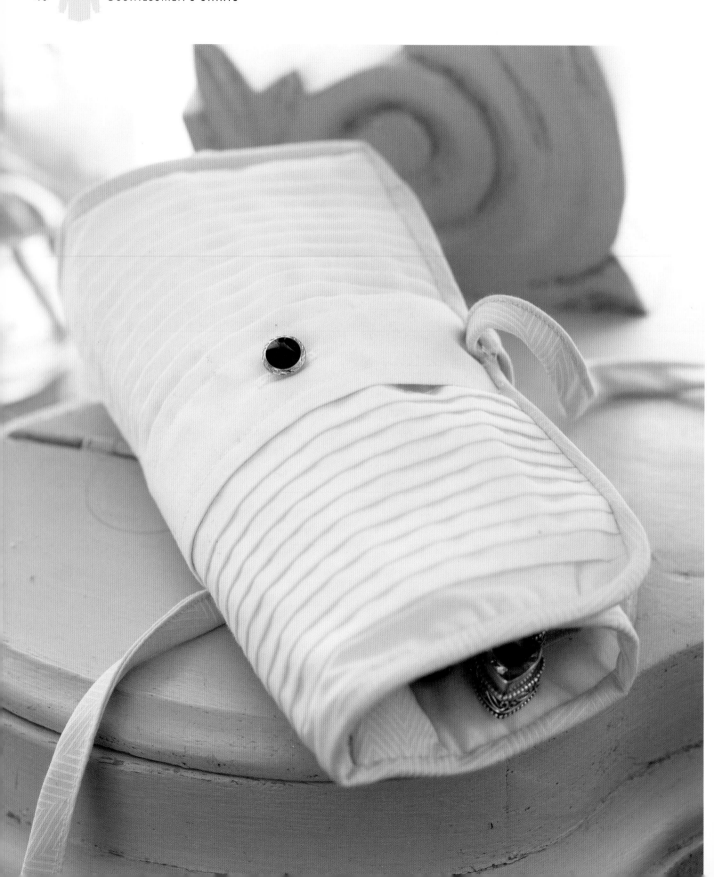

5

6 Sew one half of a press stud on the loose end of the ring pad and the other onto the jewelry roll itself so that it can be secured in place (see pic. 6).

3 To make the ring holder, cut out a piece from the contrasting shirt using the pattern. Fold the fabric piece in half lengthwise, wrong sides together, and machine stitch down the long side and one narrow end. Turn right side out and then fill with kapok or cotton wool stuffing. Sandwich the wadding between the pleated shirt front and the lining with the pockets, right sides outwards. Pin the short raw edge of the ring roll in position on the outer edge between the pockets. Pin, baste, and machine stitch all the layers together ¼ in (6 mm) from the outside edge.

4 To make the tie, cut strips of bias 1¼ in (3 cm) wide and 3½ in (9 cm) long from the contrast shirt. You might need to sew lengths together along the short edges to make the overall length. Fold in the strip by ¼ in (6 mm) on all 4 sides, then fold in half along the length.

Iron the folds. Pin, baste, and machine stitch along the 3 folded edges. Fold the finished strip in half and hand sew the fold on the front of the jewelry roll, at the top of the placket.

5 From the contrast shirt cut some bias strips ¾ in (2 cm) wide and long enough to go around all 4 sides of your mat. Again, sew lengths together if necessary. Fold in each strip by ¼ in (6 mm) on each side and iron the folds. With right sides together, pin the binding strip all around the edge of the body pieces on the pleated side. Fold the binding back on itself so it can bend around the corners, forming a small pleat. Baste and machine stitch in place. Fold the binding over the raw edges to the back of the jewelry roll. Turn under and slip stitch in place along the ironed fold line, following the line of machine stitching (see pic. 5).

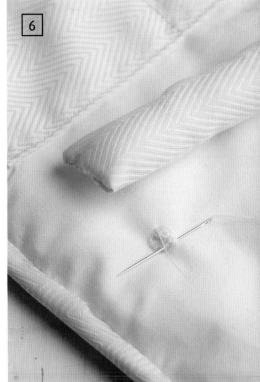

6

CREATIVE MEN'S SHIRTS

Creative men will more often than not display their creativity in their apparel, and particularly their shirts. Flamboyant in color, pattern, and fabrics, the style of the art director, architect, or ad man will shout out at you.

You can spot an architect a mile off by the cut of his shirt, most often black or white with a Nehru or Mandarin style collar and often with a placket hiding the fastenings. The brave will favor very bright colors; I turned some of these into baby booties (see pages 44–47); others prefer pattern.

The earliest form of decoration on clothing was made by printing, and fabrics patterned in this way existed long before embroidered and woven ones. Not all floral patterns are whimsical, ladylike, and tame. Strong colors, simple shapes, and powerful graphics can make them explode with glamour and richness.

The top shirt shown here is a French design made from silk, and everyone, male and female, whatever their age, who saw it when I was writing this book commented on it, touched it, and coveted it. The blue mini-floral print is very similar to a traditional Liberty fabric, although it was actually from a retail store. The tiny design is less distracting and somehow more masculine than the larger-patterned floral prints. The first shirt on the hanger is made from viscose, a fabric made from wood pulp. To make the most of its faded retro feel, I have partnered it with a classic houndstooth check in red to make some 1950s-style cushions (see pages 82–85).

I have put some of the floral shirts dating back to the sixties and seventies to good use, making a patchwork chair cover in strong and clashing patterns (see pages 56–59). I even used the cuffs as ready-made patchwork rectangles, as well as a shirt pocket on the back of a chair. Linen, another fabric loved by creatives, has been used to make a soft rabbit with very long legs (see pages 74–77).

For those of you who love classic denim, I have made a reversible bread bucket from a denim shirt and a blue-and-white floral one (see pages 86–89).

MINI ME BABY BOOTIES

These are the cutest baby booties you can find, and because they take so little fabric, you can make lots of them. I found some great plain, colored shirts so was able to mix and match the linings and the outer fabrics. If you aren't so lucky, then either dye some shirts or use patterned ones. The softer the fabric, the better for a baby's feet.

MATERIALS

- 2 different colored shirts per pair of booties
- Matching thread
- 12 in (30 cm) fusible interlining
- Paper to make patterns
- Press studs

EQUIPMENT

- Pencil
- Paper-cutting scissors
- Pins
- Dressmaking scissors
- Iron and ironing board
- Sewing machine
- Needle

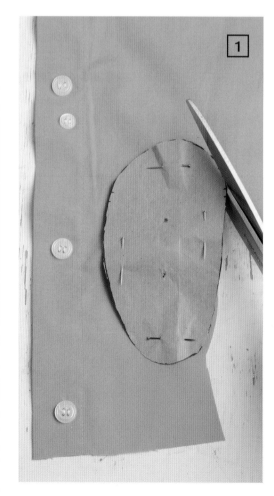

INSTRUCTIONS

1 Using paper patterns made from the templates on page 141, cut out in both the lining fabric and the outer fabric a right and left sole and two uppers of the shoe (see pic. 1). Cut out 2 of each, sole and upper, in fusible interlining.

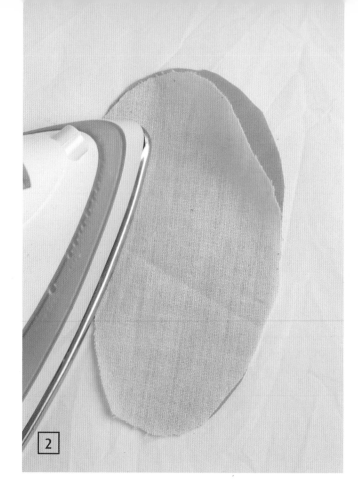

2 Iron the interlining onto the wrong sides of the sole and upper of the shoe cut from the outer fabric (see pic. 2).

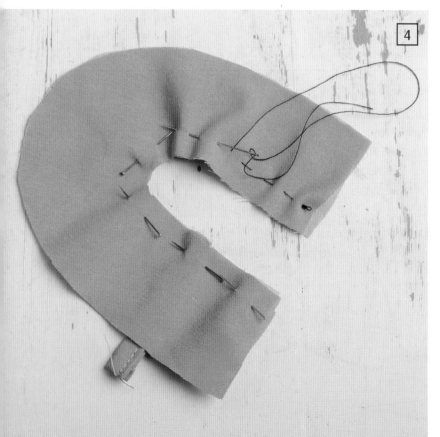

3 Cut a piece of outer fabric 2¾ x 1¾ in (7 x 4 cm) for the strap. Fold in the two short sides by ¼ in (6 mm), then fold the two long sides to the middle. Fold the strap in half lengthwise and press. Pin, baste, and machine stitch along the length of the strap.

4 With right sides together, and with the strap sandwiched between, pin and baste the lining upper onto the outer upper on the inside edge (see pic. 4). This is a curved seam so you may need to make notches at the curve to ease it.

5 Turn inside out, and, with right sides together, line up the straight back edges of the lining fabric with each other, and the straight back edges of the outer fabric. Pin, baste, and machine stitch the back seams of the outer fabric and the lining fabric. Press this seam open, and then machine stitch all around the basted, curved seam.

8

6 With right sides together, pin, baste, and machine stitch the sole cut from the outer fabric and webbing to the outer fabric upper, all the way around the curved edge. With right sides together, pin, baste, and machine stitch the sole cut from the lining fabric to the lining fabric upper, but leave the curved front of the shoe open so that you can turn it right side out.

7 Push the outer shoe through the gap in the lining so it is right side out. To close the gap in the lining, turn under the raw curved edges and slip stitch closed. Push the lining neatly into the outer of the shoe.

8 Sew one half of the press stud on the end of the strap and the other half on the shoe (see pic. 8).

TIP
These booties are very soft, but a growing baby's toes are easily damaged if they are constricted, so keep checking the fit, and if necessary, make some bigger booties.

FABRIC-WRAPPED LAMP

I love this project for many reasons, including the fact that the shirts are so bright and beautiful. I decided to cover a lamp that had been hanging around for the last 15 years, and which looked very dated. Originally, I was going to use a textile hardener used for draping cloth for sculpture, but I then remembered blind stiffener, which I had successfully used for lamp-making years ago. It is readily available and very easy to use. This is a messy process so wear old clothes and protect your work surface with a plastic cloth. You may want to wear plastic or rubber gloves so you don't get too sticky.

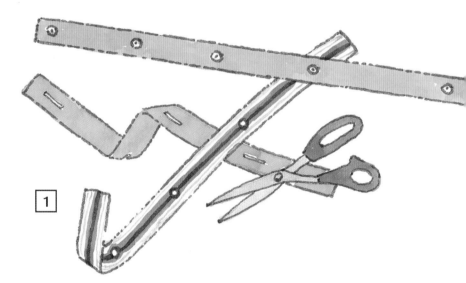

MATERIALS

- As many bright and interesting shirts as you can lay your hands on —they don't have to be whole shirts, you can use up bits left over from other projects

- A lamp—I chose a floor lamp but you could use a table lamp with a ceramic base

- A lamp shade

EQUIPMENT

- Dressmaking scissors

- 2 pots of fabric stiffener for blinds

- Plastic bag or sheeting

- Spray-on fire retardant for fabric (used mainly in the theatre but now available online)

INSTRUCTIONS

1 Roughly cut some fabric strips about 2 in (5 cm) wide. It could be more or less. I found lengths between 12 and 20 in (30 and 50 cm) were easy to work with. You can also use shirt plackets. Lay a strip on the plastic sheeting and pour some of the stiffener along the length of it. Rub the stiffener into the fabric and then lift the placket up and run your fingers down it so that the whole placket is covered in stiffener and is soaking wet.

TIP

I find if you cut fabric on the cross it gives it a malleability and stretch that it would not have otherwise. I kept the studs on one placket, and the buttons on another, and they make a nice decorative feature.

2 Start at the top of the lamp stand and wind and twist the placket around the stand. It doesn't matter if you twist it back on itself, but you must press it firmly in place to follow the contours of the lamp stand. Repeat this process with other strips of fabric and plackets until all but the base of the lamp stand is covered.

2

5 The method for covering the shade is much the same as for the base, but this time you can use random bits of shirt in different shapes. You can lay them flat, or twist them before you start applying them to give a ruched effect. To finish the shade, cut individual motifs out of unique shirt patterns—I used flowers and fish. These can be placed on top of the other fabrics to give a more finished and richer look. Leave the shade to dry overnight and then spray on the fire retardant, following the manufacturer's instructions.

3

3 To cover the base, cut triangles slightly longer than the base. Lay them around the base to make sure you have enough. You can then cut away the pointed ends of the triangles so they will fit easily around the post.

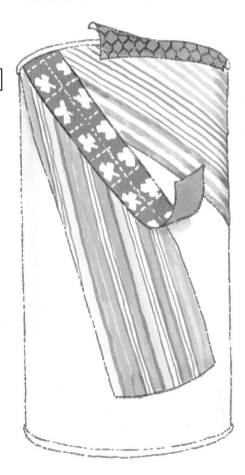

5

4 Repeat the process of soaking the fabric triangles as in step 1, and then start laying the glued pieces around the base. Cut notches on the curved edges, then tuck them under the base. Leave to dry.

4

BUTTON-DOWN SHIRT APRON

Cook up a storm with this shirt-fronted apron. This is a great way to create a masculine version of a feminine garment, but if you still find pink too pretty for the boys, then make it in a more masculine blue check as I have done on the following page. Use as large a shirt as possible for the greatest coverage and the most practical benefit.

MATERIALS

- A large shirt with a button-down collar
- Matching thread
- 60 in (1.5 m) white cotton tape

EQUIPMENT

- Tape measure
- Tailors' chalk
- Dressmaking scissors
- Sewing machine
- Pins
- Needle

INSTRUCTIONS

1 Lay the shirt on a flat surface and measure 8 in (20 cm) down the shirt front from the neck and 4¾ in (12 cm) away from the central placket. Mark this point with tailors' chalk. Mark a similar point 4¾ in (12 cm) from the placket on the other side of the shirt. These points indicate the bib front of the apron. Draw curved lines from the neck, through the marked points and out to the sides. Cut through both the front and back and along the lines to remove the sleeves (see pic. 1).

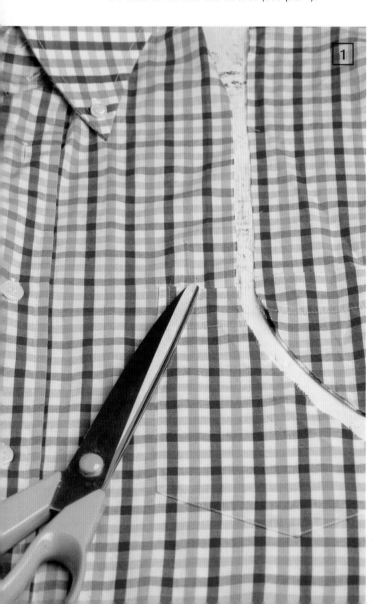

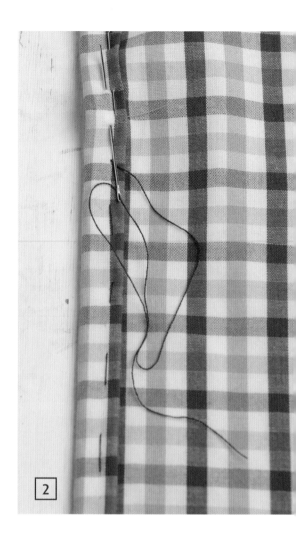

2 Turn the shirt over and draw 2 lines, the first ¾ in (2 cm) below the collar and the second 17 in (43 cm) below the collar. Cut away the top of the shirt between the lines. Cut a line up the center back of the shirt and then open up the shirt. At the collar, turn under the raw edge by ½ in (1 cm) twice and pin, baste, and machine stitch, so all you see at the top of the apron is a collar. Turn under the raw edges on the apron by ½ in (1 cm) twice and pin, baste, and machine stitch. Top stitch over this seam to stop the curved edges from curling in (see pic. 2).

3 Cut 2 lengths of 30 in (76 cm) of white tape. Turn under one end, pin, and then sew them on as apron ties to the top corners of each side of the apron back (see pic. 3).

TIP
Aprons will, of course, get dirty, so choose shirts that can withstand frequent washing, such as cotton.

PATCHWORK CHAIR

This project brings together some wonderfully patterned men's shirts, in amazing fabrics and textures to create a stunning chair cover. The chair, a real find, was a fixture from a shop on the King's Road in London's Chelsea that was closing down. Originally, the chair was covered in a washed-out salmon pink fabric that resembled old ladies' corsetry! I hope you agree that the transformation was worth it. Unless you wish to get into upholstery, don't attempt this project if the chair you wish to cover is falling to pieces. If it is only the cover that needs replacing, the project is feasible and fun.

MATERIALS

- Shirt remnants in different colors and patterns
- Matching thread
- Paper to make patterns
- Upholstery tacks
- Decorative upholstery nails

EQUIPMENT

- Needle-nosed pliers
- Pins
- Pencil
- Paper-cutting scissors
- Dressmaking scissors
- Sewing machine
- Iron and ironing board
- Small pin hammer

INSTRUCTIONS

1 Make patterns for your new patchwork covers from the old covers. Using the needle-nosed pliers, pry out the old upholstery nails and tacks. Carefully remove the fabric, observing just how it was fitted to your chair. Pin the pieces right side up on the paper and draw around them. Cut out your patterns.

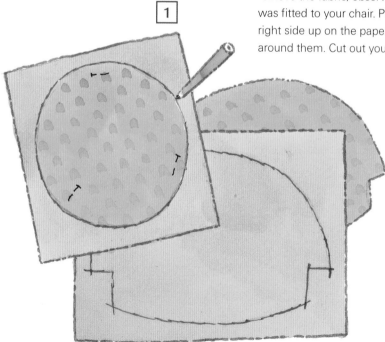

2 Choose your fabrics. You may only have a small remnant of a shirt or even just a cuff, but you can use it here as the patchwork is so random. Machine stitch any button holes closed with a zigzag stitch and sew patches behind any pockets before you start. Create sections of patchwork by machine stitching oblongs or even irregular shapes to one another. Try to use the sturdier fabrics at the edges, where you will be doing most of the pulling and tacking. Iron all seams flat.

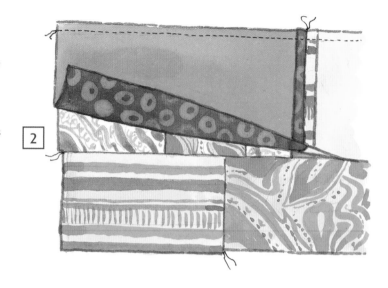

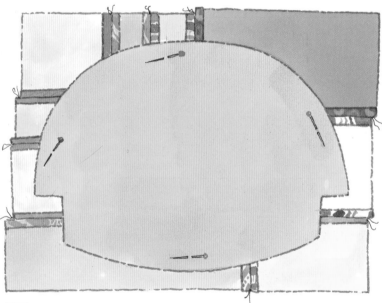

3 Pin your paper patterns on your sections of patchwork, allowing at least 2 in (5 cm) seam allowance all the way around each piece. Lay each patchwork section onto the chair to see how it looks, and to be sure you are happy with the overall design before cutting out the shapes.

4 Pin each section onto the chair. You can then start attaching the pieces using upholstery tacks. Start with the back of the chair. Begin in the middle and work outwards, stretching and pulling as you go. Apply a tack every 1¼ in (3 cm). Pull the fabric so it is as taut as possible before you put in the tacks. When you have reached one end, go back to the middle and start again, working in the opposite direction.

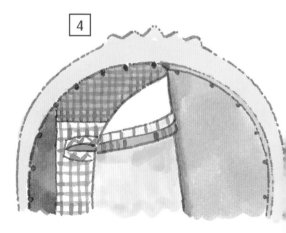

5 Repeat this process to attach the other patchwork pieces. Always work from a center point outwards, applying tacks in one direction and then the opposite direction, so that you don't get twisting and distortion. Check that you are happy with your work as you go, and make adjustments as necessary. To finish, hammer the decorative upholstery nails around the edge of the chair, covering the tacks you previously hammered in.

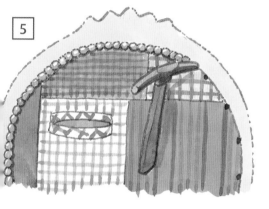

TIP
If a shirt fabric you want to use is very thin and fine, iron it onto fusible interlining to give it some strength.

GINGHAM SACHETS

This project is made by using shirt pockets to create lavender and herb sachets to hang in your closet or store between your blankets. By using natural repellents, such as thyme, southernwood, wormwood, tansy, cloves, and rosemary, you can repel moths. Or, just use lavender to make your linen smell delightful.

MATERIALS

- Gingham shirts
- Matching thread
- Dried lavender or other dried herbs

EQUIPMENT

- Seam ripper
- Dressmaking scissors
- Iron and ironing board
- Pins
- Sewing machine

INSTRUCTIONS

1 Carefully unpick the shirt pocket from the shirt and iron the existing seam flat so a pattern is created using the pocket with the addition of the seam allowance. Pin the flattened pocket onto another section of the shirt and, using it as a pattern, cut out a back for the herb sachet (see pic. 1).

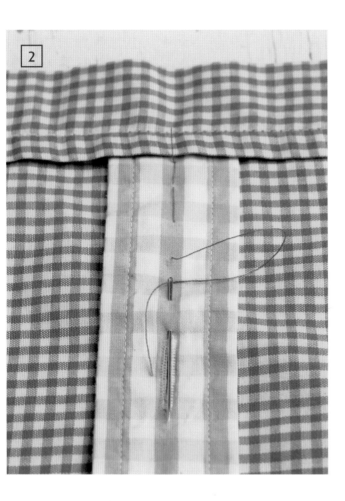

3 With right sides facing in, pin, baste, and machine stitch the two pieces of fabric together nearly all the way around. Leave enough room to turn the sachet right side out. Turn the right side out and press flat. Fill either with dried lavender on its own or a mixture of the herbs suggested in the introduction. When it is tightly packed with herbs, slip stitch the opening closed (see pic. 3).

2 If you wish to show the fabric origins, cut a piece of placket, either from the same shirt or a contrasting one, and pin then baste it onto the front of the bag down the center (see pic. 2). Machine stitch in place.

TIP

Other ideas for decorating the lavender bags include re-using shirt buttons and sewing them in a line along one edge, sewing buttons on as a motif, for example a star shape, or using a collar tip to create a point of interest.

FOLDING CHAIR COVERS

This is a great project to make if you have a few shirts in either complementary or contrasting fabrics. I was lucky enough to find floral shirts in similar colors but with different scale patterns, as well as some striped and checked shirts in the same color schemes. I used the striped shirts to make the piping. This is a project that works well with a small amount of fabric in one of the patterns. If you have only the sleeves of a shirt these will probably be wide enough to make a frill.

MATERIALS

- 2 or 3 floral or patterned shirts in similar color schemes but different designs
- Matching thread
- Paper to make patterns
- Pillow cushion
- Cord for binding

EQUIPMENT

- Tape measure
- Pencil
- Paper-cutting scissors
- Pins
- Dressmaking scissors
- Needle
- Sewing machine
- Iron and ironing board
- Tailors' chalk

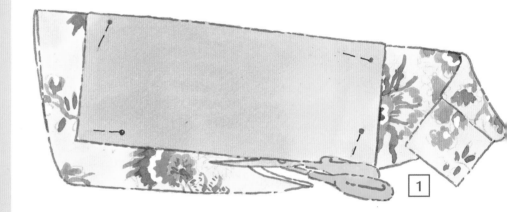

INSTRUCTIONS

1 Measure the chair back and the chair seat, and add a ½ in (1 cm) seam allowance all the way around. Make a paper pattern to these measurements. Decide which shirts you want for which parts of the covers. Choose the largest shirt for the seat cover and put it to the side. Pin the chair back pattern onto another shirt—you should be able to cut this in one piece out of a shirt sleeve, using the fold for the top seam.

TIP

Bias binding is a way of neatening an edge with a contrasting fabric. Fabrics cut on the cross are pliable, so they can be used on both straight and curved edges.

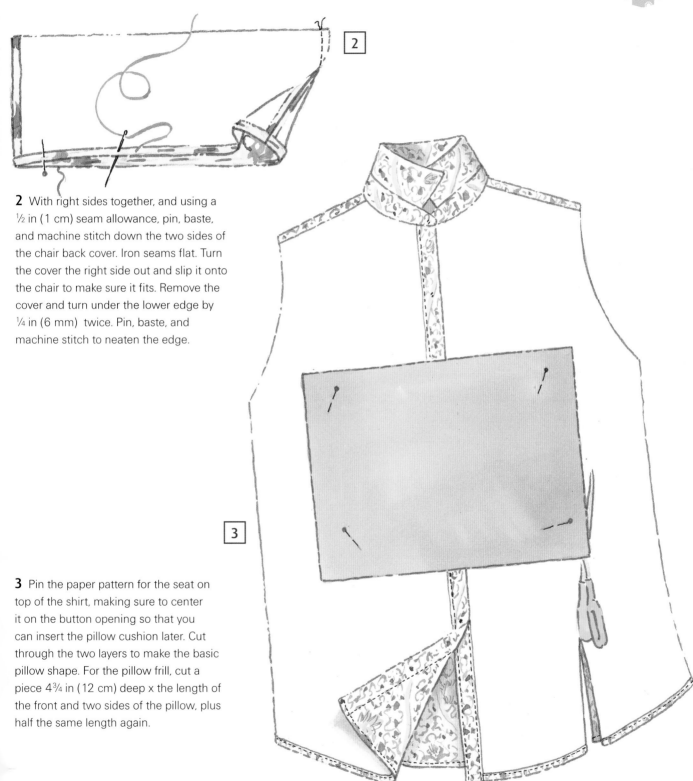

2 With right sides together, and using a ½ in (1 cm) seam allowance, pin, baste, and machine stitch down the two sides of the chair back cover. Iron seams flat. Turn the cover the right side out and slip it onto the chair to make sure it fits. Remove the cover and turn under the lower edge by ¼ in (6 mm) twice. Pin, baste, and machine stitch to neaten the edge.

3 Pin the paper pattern for the seat on top of the shirt, making sure to center it on the button opening so that you can insert the pillow cushion later. Cut through the two layers to make the basic pillow shape. For the pillow frill, cut a piece 4¾ in (12 cm) deep x the length of the front and two sides of the pillow, plus half the same length again.

4 Using a shirt with a contrast pattern to that of the main seat cover, make bias binding strips. Fold the bottom edge of the front of the contrasting shirt up to the side and cut along this diagonal line. Draw a second line parallel with the cut edge ¾ in (2 cm) away and cut a strip. Repeat this process until you have cut enough bias for the project, joining strips with a diagonal seam. Iron these seams flat.

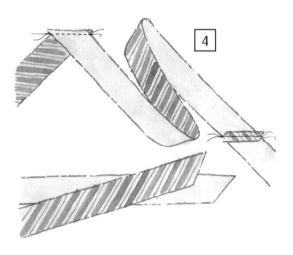

4

5

5 Fold the bias binding in half around the binding cord lengthwise, with the right side outwards. Pin and baste to close, then machine stitch. Wrap the piping around the sides and front of the fabric for the top of the pillow cover, right side up, lining up the raw edges. Pin into position. Make a small cut in the seam allowance of the bias binding to help it turn the corners neatly.

6 To make two chair ties, cut 2 pieces 1¼ x 16 in (3 x 41 cm) from a contrasting shirt. Fold in all the raw edges by ¼ in (6 mm), then pin, baste, and machine stitch. Fold each tie in half and pin and baste in place 1¾ in (4 cm) from the back corners of the seat cover.

8 With right sides together, pin the back of the pillow cover over the front, undoing the buttons first. Sandwich the frill, ties, and bias between the two layers. Pin, baste, and machine stitch around all four sides, taking care not to stitch over the cord in the bias binding. Turn the cover right side out through the opening, insert the pillow cushion, fasten the buttons, and tie the pillow to the chair. Slip the chair back in place, too.

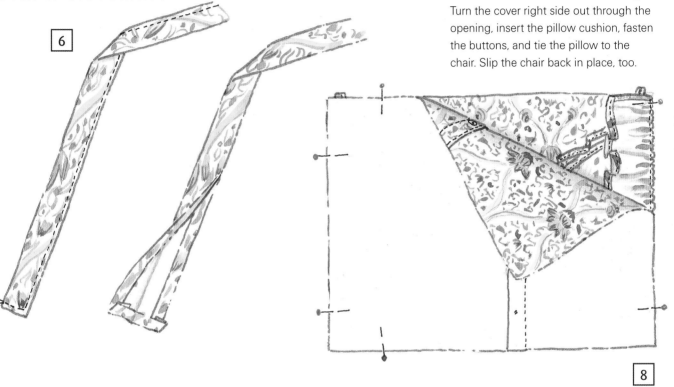

6

8

7 To neaten the two short sides and one long side of the frill, fold in the raw edges by 1/16 in (2 mm) twice. Pin, baste, and machine stitch. Hand-sew a line of gathering stitches along the raw edge of the frill. Tighten the gathering stitches and, with right sides facing out, adjust the frill to fit over the bias around the two sides and front of the chair cushion. Pin the frill in place as you work. Baste and machine stitch in place.

7

HOT COFFEE COVER

How to overcome cold coffee syndrome? Make a coffee cozy. This one for a cafetière is made from two differently colored gingham fabrics, so it is reversible. The Velcro is sewn on both sides, so it is easy to fasten whichever way around the cafetière it is worn. Make sure the shirt you choose is cotton and machine washable, in case of spills and stains.

MATERIALS

- 2 different gingham shirts
- Matching thread
- Velcro
- Wadding
- Paper to make a pattern

EQUIPMENT

- Tape measure
- Pencil
- Paper-cutting scissors
- Sewing machine
- Dressmaking scissors
- Iron and ironing board
- Needle

INSTRUCTIONS

1 Measure the circumference of the cafetière, add ¾ in (2 cm) for the fastening and ½ in (1 cm) for seam allowance. Measure the height of the pot from just above the pouring spout to the bottom of the glass. Add ½ in (1 cm) for seam allowance.

2 Using these dimensions, draw a rectangle onto paper. Fit this around the cafetière—it will be bigger all around. Fold the paper pattern in half and cut a V shape to a depth of about 1¼ in (3 cm) in the center; the width of the V should be about 2 in (5 cm). Cut away a half semicircle at each corner of the rectangular pattern. These should be 1¼ in (2.5 cm) high, and 2 in (5 cm) wide (see pic. 2).

3 Wrap the pattern around the cafetière and make any adjustments necessary (see pic. 3).

TIP

Use the same method as the one shown here for making mug warmers or milk jug warmers.

4 Use the pattern to cut the outer and the inner fabric pieces and the wadding. (see pic. 4). Machine stitch the wadding to the wrong side of the outer fabric, all the way around the edge. With right sides together, machine stitch the backing fabric onto the outer fabric piece nearly all the way around, leaving one of the short sides open.

5 Trim into the V shape and the curves, cutting away any excess fabric. Turn the cover the right side out and turn the raw edges under on the open side. Press flat using an iron, and top stitch all the way around the cafetière cover ⅛ in (3 mm) from the edge.

6 Pin and baste the Velcro strip so that the softer piece runs down one short side of one fabric side, and the hooked rougher piece is on the reverse fabric, on the opposite end of the cover (see pic. 6). Press together around the cafetière to check that it fits and machine stitch.

FLOPPY RABBIT

This rabbit is made from a pale linen striped shirt. She has long floppy ears and is wearing red check trousers, a striped shirt, and cuffs. Her shirt is made from one shirt and her trousers another. Lovely as she is, she is not designed for very young children to play with, as there are too many small pieces that could get lost, chewed, or, even worse, swallowed.

MATERIALS

- 1 linen shirt
- 2 patterned shirts
- Matching thread
- Paper to make patterns
- 4 buttons taken from one of the shirts for the cuffs and the shirt
- 2 smaller shirt buttons for the eyes
- Kapok or soft toy stuffing
- 8 in (20 cm) elastic, ¼ in (6 mm) wide for the trousers

EQUIPMENT

- Pencil
- Paper-cutting scissors
- Pins
- Dressmaking scissors
- Sewing machine
- Needle
- Iron and ironing board

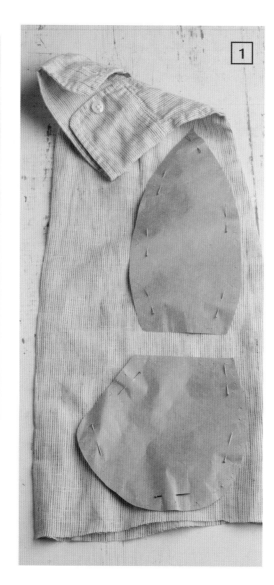

INSTRUCTIONS

1 Using the templates on page 140 to make paper patterns, cut 4 ear shapes and 2 head shapes from the linen shirt (see pic. 1). For the legs cut 2 rectangles 5½ x 9½ in (14 x 24 cm). Cut 2 more rectangles the same size for the long arms. The body is made by cutting 2 rectangles 5 x 8¼ in (13 x 21 cm).

2 With right sides together, pin, baste, and machine stitch the 2 head pieces together, leaving the bottom open. Turn right side out and press. For the legs, fold each rectangle in half, then, with right sides together, pin, baste, and machine stitch along one short side, forming a rounded end, and one long side, leaving one short side open. Trim the excess fabric around the curve, turn right side out through the opening and press. Make the 2 arms in the same way. Fill the head arms, and legs with stuffing.

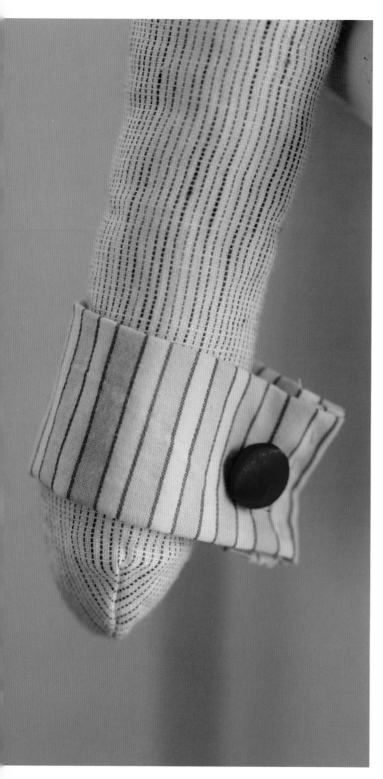

3 With right sides together, pin and baste the open ends of the arms to the back body section. Pin and baste the legs into place. Pin and baste the front body section over the top, right sides together, trapping the arms and legs between. Machine stitch around all sides except the neck edge. This will be a bit tight but they will all fit. Turn the body right side out—the arms and legs will be sticking out. Fill the body with stuffing.

4 Sew loose gathering stitches along the neck edge of the head. Draw the threads tight to close. Sew each ear front to each back, leaving the bottom edge open, and turn right side out. Turn under the raw edge, slip stitch closed, and press. Make a fold in the bottom of the ears. Pin and then slip stitch them to the top of the head (see pic.4).

7 To make the trousers, cut 2 pieces from the second patterned shirt 12½ x 7½ in (32 x 19 cm). To form the legs of the trousers, fold each piece in half and cut up the fold, leaving 4 in (10 cm) uncut. With right sides facing out, pin, baste, and machine stitch the trouser front to the trouser back down the side seams and around the inside legs. Fold over the top and pin, baste, and machine stitch to make a ½ in (1 cm) casing, leaving a small hole to thread the elastic through. Fit the trousers onto the rabbit, rolling up the bottom of the legs.

8 Make a scarf from a piece of the same shirt measuring 14 x 1¼ in (35 x 3 cm). Fold in half with right sides together. Pin, baste, and machine stitch down 1 long and 1 short side. Turn through and slip stitch the end closed. Tie jauntily around the rabbit's neck.

5 Hand sew the head onto the body (see pic. 5). Sew a button on either side of the head for eyes. To make the shirt: follow the instructions for the teddy bear nightshirt (see pages 24–25.) Fit the shirt onto the rabbit.

6 Make the rabbit's cuff by cutting two pieces of contrasting fabric, each measuring 8 x 2¾ in (20 x 7 cm). With right sides together, fold in half then pin, baste, and machine stitch around 1 short and 1 long edge. Turn right side out, press, and then slip stich the opening closed. Fold the cuff, slip it over the rabbit's arm and pin (see pic. 6). Sew a button in place to hold the cuff on the rabbit. Repeat for the other cuff.

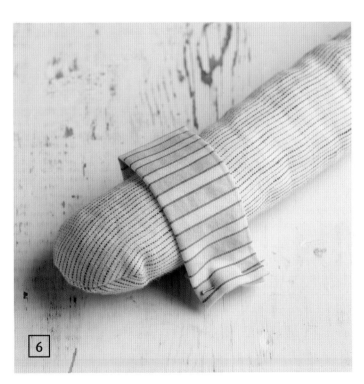

BEACH BUM BAG

I chose to turn this shirt into a beach bag because of its exuberant floral fabric embellished with glitter, silver thread, beads, and diamanté buttons. I then found a white silk shirt with a brightly colored fish design—the perfect lining fabric. For your bag, try to find the wildest shirts you can. Remember the size of your bag will be governed by the size of the shirt, so the bigger the better.

MATERIALS

- 2 shirts with wild designs, with pockets
- Matching thread

EQUIPMENT

- Seam ripper
- Dressmaking scissors
- Tape measure
- Sewing machine

INSTRUCTIONS

1 Unpick the pocket from the shirt you want to use for the outside of the bag and put it to the side. With the two front edges touching, fold the shirt in half. Cut across the shirt from the point where the sleeves join the body. Discard the top of the shirt.

2 Turn the shirt through 90 degrees so the fastenings are now at the top of what will be the bag. From this fabric cut two rectangles 16½ x 14 in (42 x 35 cm). If you want a bigger bag, make these measurements larger.

TIP

If you want an internal pocket on your bag, sew a pocket to the right side of one of the pieces you are using to make your lining before you sew the two pieces together.

3 Pin, baste, and machine stitch the pocket to the right side of one of the pieces of fabric. With right sides together, pin, baste, and machine stitch the front of the bag to the back along the 2 sides and bottom. The top edge will be formed by the shirt plackets.

5 Make the lining from the second shirt in the same way as you did the outer bag, but without the plackets. Allow an extra ¾ in (2 cm) at the top so you can turn over the raw edge. Insert the lining and slip stitch it to the outer shell.

4 Cut two pieces of fabric from the same shirt measuring 3 x 26 in (8 x 66 cm)—you might need to join pieces to get a long enough strip. Fold the strips in half and turn the long edges in by ½ in (1 cm). Press flat. Machine stitch down each side with a running stitch and down the middle with a zigzag stitch. Pin the handles onto the bag and then sew them into position using a running stitch. To give the handles extra strength, sew a cross where the handle fits onto the bag.

FIFTIES-INSPIRED PILLOWS

I saw a pillow similar to these at a vintage clothing market and was so inspired I decided to make one or two for this book. It is a great way of using up remnants of shirting. I have only used two shirts for each pillow but you could go really wild if you chose to and use lots of different fabrics in one pillow.

MATERIALS

- 2 shirts
- Matching thread
- Paper to make patterns
- A large button
- Pillow cushion

EQUIPMENT

- Tape measure
- Paper-cutting scissors
- Pencil
- Needle
- Pins
- Dressmaking scissors
- Sewing machine

3

INSTRUCTIONS

1 It is very easy to make a pattern for this pillow. Cut 2 squares of paper to the dimension of your pillow cushion, allowing an extra ½ in (1cm) all the way around for seam allowance.

2 Put one of the pattern pieces to one side to use for the pillow back. To make the pattern for the pillow front, draw a pencil line showing the seam allowance all around the edge. Then fold the pattern piece into quarters and cut. You will now have 4 small squares. Fold each of them in half across the diagonal and cut again, making 8 triangles. You will need to add ½ in (1 cm) seam allowance on the diagonal edges. I found the easiest way to do this was to cut a new triangle pattern with the added seam allowance.

3 Using the square pattern cut the back piece from one shirt. Cut 4 triangles from the same shirt and 4 from the second shirt (see pic. 3).

4

4 With right sides facing out, pin, baste, and machine stitch one triangular piece onto a different designed triangular piece along the long side (see pic. 4). You will end up with 4 squares. Sew the 4 squares together to make one large square the size of the pillow back.

6 Sew the large button into the center of the pillow where all the triangles meet (see pic. 6). If you want to form an indent, sew through to the back of the pillow and pull the thread hard.

5 Place the pillow back on top of the pillow front, right sides together, and pin and then baste in place. Machine stitch around 3 sides and half of the fourth side. Turn out to the right side. Insert the pillow cushion through the opening and then slip stitch to close the gap (see pic. 5).

BREAD BUCKET

This reversible bread bucket is made from two contrasting shirts, a heavyweight dark denim and a fine white cotton with a blue flowery print. The fabric has been stiffened with interlining to give it body and prevent the sides from collapsing. Curved seams need to be stitched with care, so that the seam allowance remains the same all around. Once the seam has been stitched, notches should be cut into the seam allowance at regular intervals, so that the seam can be ironed flat for a neat finish.

MATERIALS

- A flowery shirt
- A denim shirt
- Matching thread
- Paper to make patterns
- 20 in (50 cm) fusible interlining

EQUIPMENT

- Compass or a plate to draw around
- Pencil
- Ruler
- Tape measure
- Paper-cutting scissors
- Seam ripper
- Pins
- Dressmaking scissors
- Sewing machine
- Iron and ironing board

MAKING THE PAPER PATTERN

1 Either use a pencil and compass to draw a circle with a diameter of $8\frac{7}{8}$ in (22.5 cm) onto the pattern paper, or draw around a plate of your chosen size. Cut the paper circle out.

2 Calculate the circumference of the circle —either measure the diameter and multiply by pi (3.142), or fold the circle into quarters and measure a quarter, then multiply by 4; add $\frac{3}{4}$ in (2 cm) for the seam allowance. This measurement is the length of the strip of shirt fabric needed for the sides of the cylinder. If the diameter of the circle is $8\frac{7}{8}$ in (22.5 cm), the measurement will be $27\frac{3}{4}$ in (70.5 cm) + $\frac{3}{4}$ in (2 cm) seam allowance = $28\frac{1}{2}$ in (72.5 cm). The height of the cylinder shown here is $6\frac{3}{4}$ in (17 cm) including seam allowances. Cut a paper pattern for the sides of the bucket $28\frac{1}{2}$ x $6\frac{3}{4}$ in (72.5 x 17 cm).

INSTRUCTIONS

1 If you have a fitted shirt like the floral one used here, you will need to unpick the darts in the bodice (see pic. 1).

1

2 Starting with the denim shirt, pin the pattern pieces onto the shirt to make sure you have enough fabric. If you can't get a long enough piece of fabric for the sides of the cylinder, you may have to join two strips together, so don't forget to add seam allowances for this.

3 Cut out a square of fabric around the circle pattern for the base. Remove the paper pattern and then, following the manufacturer's instructions, iron the interlining onto the wrong side of the denim. Pin the circle pattern onto the denim and cut out the base (see pic. 3).

4 Cut out the strip(s) of denim for the sides of the bucket and iron interlining onto the wrong side (see pic. 4).

5 With right sides facing out, pin and then machine stitch the two ends of the strip together with a ⅜ in (1 cm) seam allowance. Press the seam open.

6 With right sides facing out, pin the circular base to one long edge of the strip. Pin at regular intervals, with the pins positioned at right angles to the edge. Baste together and then machine stitch with a ½ in (1 cm) seam allowance, feeding the fabric through the machine and guiding it around the curved edge. Cut notches into the seam allowance at regular intervals and press flat.

7 Repeat steps 2 to 6 to make a second bucket using the floral fabric.

8 Insert the floral bucket into the denim bucket with wrong sides together. Turn the raw top edges of both buckets ½ in (1 cm) to the inside, and then machine stitch the buckets together with a line of top stitching along the edge (see pic. 8). Fold over the edge of the finished bucket.

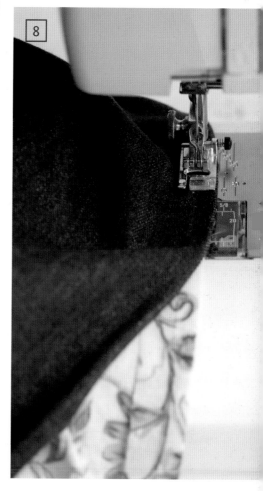

OUTDOORSY MEN'S SHIRTS

Outdoor shirts is the general term applied to working men's shirts. Often made from a thick plaid or tartan, known as lumberjack shirts, they are durable, comfortable, and functional. Historically this meant they needed to be wind and rainproof. Tartan is a closely woven fabric and is very durable when made from wool, which makes it naturally water resistant as well as warm. In order for a piece of cloth to be known as tartan, it has to be a twill weave. A twill is where the weft threads cross over two and then under two warp threads, creating the effect of a diagonal rib. The "sett"— the number and order of colors which make up the pattern—follows a strict order.

It was reported in *The New York Times* that after 9/11 a lot of New Yorkers started wearing tartan shirts, almost as a way of regaining what they knew and loved—they were viewed as safe, warm, and comforting garments.

Check and plaid is worn by a huge percentage of the American population at the moment. The two most stylish makers are Pendelton and the British Harris Tweed. The popularity of the Pendelton shirt among American youth began during the 1960s when a pop group took the name "The Pendletones." The group later changed their name to the Beach Boys and, as they say, the rest is history.

Denim is another fabric traditionally used for working men's shirts. Originally they were reserved for cowboys, who still buy them untreated, so that they are rigid and stiff when new. Both denim and plaid shirts have now become fashion items. However, real cowboy shirts can be distinguished by the fact that they are made without a hem to prevent abrasion in the saddle.

Wanting to make use of the durability of outdoor shirts, I created a garden organizer using a twill-weave fisherman's smock and some plaid shirts (see pages 100–103). In complete contrast, I made a clutch bag using small scale plaid in contrasting colors (see pages 110–113). Corduroy is another durable fabric traditionally used for work shirts. I have put it to good use for a clothespin bag (see pages 96–99) and some stylish place mats (see pages 104–107).

OWL DOORSTOP

Lumberjack shirts, with their bold checks and homespun feel, really lend themselves to this project. In addition to the lumberjack shirts, use corners cut off collars from all of your shirt projects. Even the owl's beak is cut from the very tip of a collar. I filled the doorstop with rice as it is very malleable and yet heavy enough to do the job. You can use other grains or even sand.

MATERIALS

- 1 lumberjack shirt for the body, plus the cuffs from another shirt
- 26 collar tips, including two yellow ones for the feet
- Matching thread
- White felt for the eyes
- 2 flat beads and 2 tiny beads
- Yellow tapestry wool
- Paper to make a pattern
- Large bag of rice

EQUIPMENT

- Pencil
- Paper-cutting scissors
- Dressmaking scissors
- Needle
- Tapestry needle
- Sewing machine

INSTRUCTIONS

1 Using the templates on pages 136–137, cut two body shapes and one base. Lay 5 collar tips in a curve halfway down the body—place the first one centrally then overlap it on either side. Pin, baste, and machine stitch them in place, then go over the stitched line using a zigzag stitch. Hold these feathers up, and pin collar tips in the spaces between the first row of feathers to form a second row. Repeat until the bottom half of the owl's front is covered.

2 To form the beak, cut the tip off a collar, pin, and then machine stitch it on the owl using zigzag stitch. To make the eyes, cut two circles from white felt. Sew a flat bead to the center and anchor it using a tiny bead, or sew a button into the center of each circle. Pin the eyes onto the owl then, using the tapestry needle and thread, overstitch the eyes onto the front of the owl.

TIP
Collect as many different designs and colors of collar tip as you can. If you have enough, use them on the back as well as on the front of the owl.

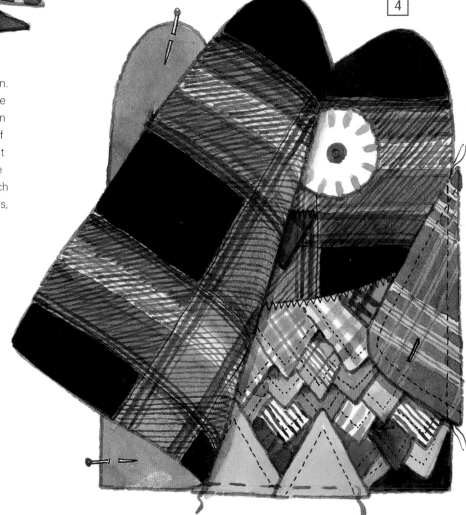

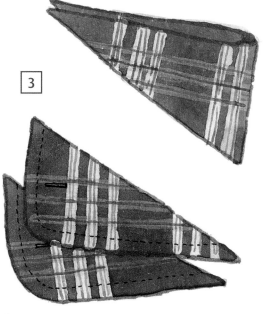

4 With right sides facing in, pin and baste the front and the back pieces together, sandwiching the wings in between. Insert the base piece and pin and baste the front piece to the front half of the base, sandwiching the feet between the front and base pieces. Machine stitch all seams. Turn the owl right side out through the gap. Turn the owl upside down and fill with rice. To close up the gap, tuck the raw edges under, pin, and then oversew by hand the rest of the base onto the back piece.

3 To make the wings, cut a cuff from the second shirt and remove the button. Fold the cuff in half and then cut on the diagonal to form two curved pieces. Pin and baste the wings to the right side of the front piece of the owl, lining the cut edge of the wings with the edge of the body piece. Pin and then machine stitch two yellow collar tips, pointing upwards, to the center bottom of the owl front.

CLOTHESPIN BAG

Corduroy is a strong, closely woven fabric, so it is ideal for making a clothespin bag that will get a great deal of use. The brown corduroy shirt I had looked a little dull, so I embellished it with the fabric from a floral shirt in brown, green, and white and added a simple flower appliquéd motif. I used two sleeves for my clothespin bag left over from another project, joining them with a seam at the back. If you have a large enough section of shirt you can make it in one piece, so you will only need to sew up the sides.

MATERIALS

- A corduroy or needle-cord shirt
- A floral shirt
- Matching thread
- 4 in (10 cm) fusible webbing
- Wooden coat hanger

EQUIPMENT

- Tape measure
- Small saw
- Dressmaking scissors
- Scalpel or craft knife
- Pins
- Sewing machine
- Iron and ironing board
- Needle

INSTRUCTIONS

1 Either use a child's coat hanger or, as I did here, saw off some of the length from either end of a normal width wooden coat hanger. My coat hanger ended up being 11 in (28 cm) long. Cut the sleeve off your cord shirt, and then cut it again so it is 1¾ in (4 cm) longer than the coat hanger (see pic. 1).

2 Using a scalpel or craft knife, carefully make a hole centered in the sleeve seam just big enough to insert the hook of the coat hanger. Remove the coat hanger from the sleeve section and cut the sleeve so it is 4 in (10 cm) from the hole for the hook to the bottom edge, both front and back.

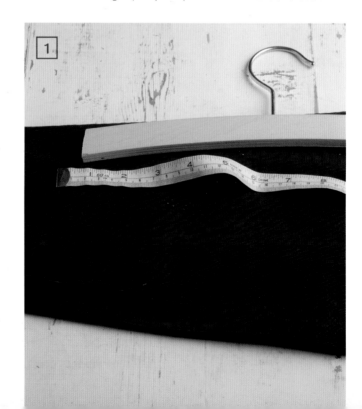

3 Cut a 2 in (5 cm) wide strip of floral shirt and with right sides together and using a ½ in (1 cm) seam allowance, pin, baste, and machine stitch the strip along the bottom front edge of the sleeve section. Fold the floral strip in half along its length and then fold under again to hide the raw edge. Iron the folded strip and then machine stitch the folded strip in place. You will now have a bound edge.

4 Cut a piece of corduroy from the other sleeve the same width as the piece you have just sewn x 12½ in (32 cm). With right sides together pin, baste, and machine stitch the unbound edge of the first piece to the top edge of the piece you have just cut. Cut another 2 in (5 cm) strip of floral shirt and neaten the raw edge of the second corduroy piece in the same way as in step 3.

5 Iron the fusible webbing onto a piece of floral shirt. Draw a simple flower design on it and cut out the elements (see pic. 5.) Fold the peg bag so that the hole for the hanger is on the top edge and the two bound edges meet at the front.

6 Arrange the flower elements on the front of the bag. When you are happy with their position, iron them in place (see pic. 6). Machine stitch around the outside edge of each appliqué piece to keep them securely in place. With wrong sides together, lay the bag flat, so that the two bound edges meet. Pin, baste, and machine stitch the two side seams. Turn right side out and insert the hanger.

7 Close part of the bound edges by oversewing 1¾ in (4 cm) from either side of the opening (see pic. 7). This will prevent the bag from gaping when you hang it up with clothespins inside.

GARDEN SHED ORGANIZER

When I am gardening, I always have to keep traipsing back into the house to find things I have forgotten. I hope this is the answer—a place to keep all those small items you need when tending your garden. What better way to use a rugged lumberjack shirt that has previously been worn for outside activities and is thus made of strong material? This organizer is made from a combination of lumberjack shirts with a sailor's shirt as a backing.

MATERIALS

- A large sailor's shirt
- Parts of 4 lumberjack shirts
- Matching thread

EQUIPMENT

- Dressmaking scissors
- Seam ripper
- Tape measure
- Eyelet maker and three eyelets
- Pins
- Sewing machine
- Iron and ironing board

INSTRUCTIONS

1 Cut out a rectangle of fabric from the sailor's shirt. Make it as large as you can. It is worth undoing any hems on the bottom of the shirt as this will add to the length of the fabric. Measure up from the bottom of the curved part of a lumberjack shirt and cut off the bottom—my piece was 7 in (17 cm) at the sides rising to 8½ in (22 cm) in the middle, as the shirt had a traditional tail. Cut this piece and put to the side for later.

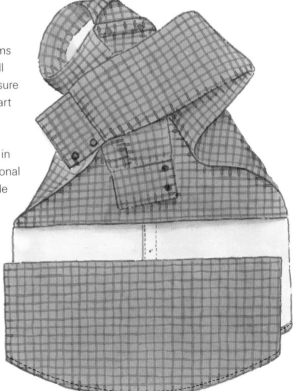

2 Unpick the pockets from 2 other lumberjack shirts. Insert an eyelet in one of them, following the manufacturer's instructions. Pin, baste, and machine stitch this pocket onto the left-hand side of the upended shirt tail.

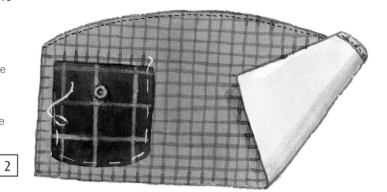

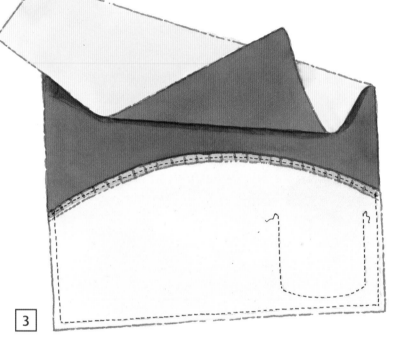

stitch vertical lines down the sides of the two loops and then on either side of the loops horizontally as near to the edge of the placket as possible. Measure down from the bottom of the first placket 5½ in (14 cm) and lay the second placket across the hanging. Make loops as you did in the first placket. Where you put them and how many there are is up to you, and will depend on what you need to hang up. Pin a large pocket 1¼ in (3 cm) from the right-hand side of the hanging and covering part of both plackets. Baste and machine stitch in place.

3 Using a ½ in (1 cm) seam allowance, pin, baste, and then machine stitch the shirt tail onto the bottom of the rectangle from the sailor's shirt. Turn right side out.

4 Cut the plackets from 3 of the lumberjack shirts. Measure down 4¾ in (12 cm) from the top of the hanging and start to pin the first placket. Place a pin 2¾ in (7 cm) from the edge and then make a loop of 2½ in (6 cm) and place another pin. Measure a further 2½ in (6 cm) and make a second loop of 1¾ in (4 cm) and mark with a pin. Pin the rest of the placket in a straight row. Machine

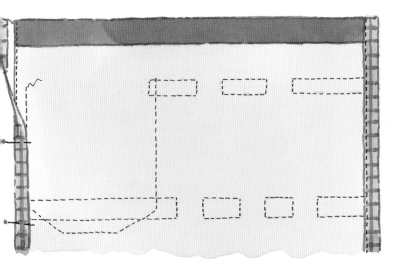

5

5 Fold the top of the hanging over ½ in (1 cm) and then a further 1¼ in (3 cm) and press flat. Cut a strip of contrast shirting 2 in (5 cm) x the length of the hanging. With right sides together and using a ¼ in (6 mm) seam allowance, pin, baste, and machine stitch the bias strip in place on the front of the hanging down one long side, tucking in the raw edges at top and bottom. Press the fold over and pin the strip to the reverse of the hanging, folding in the long raw edge. Baste and then machine stitch the binding into place. Press flat, then repeat on the edge of the other long side.

6 Divide the shirt tail pocket into three sections with two vertical lines of machine stitching. Machine stitch along the bottom edge to finish. In the top corners of the hanging, insert eyelets so you can hang up the garden organizer. Cut the remaining placket into 3 equal lengths. Fold each one in half to create a loop. Pin the loops at even intervals along the bottom of the hanging. Baste, then machine stitch in place.

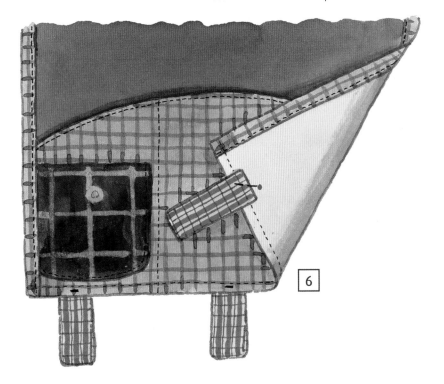

6

CORDUROY PLACE MATS

I found a wonderful black and beige shirt that I decided to use to make place mats. I wanted something contrasting to go with it, but I only had a very dull-looking beige shirt, so I dyed it bright green in the washing machine using a fabric dye. Machine-washable dyes come in a wide variety of shades, so if you can't find a shirt in the color you want for a particular project, dye any light-colored shirt and use that instead.

MATERIALS

- 2 needlecord shirts in contrasting colors
- Matching thread
- Paper to make a pattern
- Fusible interlining

EQUIPMENT

- Tape measure
- Pencil
- Paper-cutting scissors
- Pins
- Dressmaking scissors
- Needle
- Sewing machine
- Iron and ironing board

INSTRUCTIONS

1 To make a paper pattern, cut a rectangle to the size you would like your place mat plus ¾ in (2 cm) all around. The size of the mats will be governed to some degree by the size of the shirts you have. Our rectangle measured 16½ x 12½ in (42 x 32 cm). Pin the pattern onto both fabrics and the interlining and cut out (see pic. 1).

2 With the remaining fabric from one of the shirts, cut some strips on the diagonal 1¼ in (3 cm) wide and long enough to go around all 4 sides of your mat. Join the strips together diagonally along the short edges to make the length. Fold in each strip by ¼ in (6 mm) on each side and iron the folds (see pic. 2).

3 Iron the interlining to the wrong side of the green needlecord. Then, with wrong sides facing in, pin, baste, and machine stitch the two pieces of needlecord together ¼ in (6 mm) in from the edge.

4 With right sides together, pin the binding strip to the edge of the mat along one side up to the first corner. Fold the binding back on itself so it can bend around the corner, forming a mitered pleat in the binding. Continue along the remaining sides, making a pleat at each corner. Baste and then machine stitch in place with a running stitch.

5 Fold the binding over the raw edges to the other side of the mat. Turn under the folded edge of the binding and slip stitch in place along the line of machine stitching (see pic. 5).

6 To finish, slip stitch the mitered corners on the font and back of the mat to neaten them. Make other mats in the same way. You can mix and match with different shirts to make a full set.

COUNTRY CHECK STORAGE BOXES

An elegant and inexpensive storage solution, shoe boxes come in a variety of sizes and are free, but ugly, so why not personalize them by covering them in brightly checked shirt fabrics and line them in contrasting colors? To give a neat and luxurious padded finish, the lids of each box have a piece of wadding stuck onto them before they are covered. If you want a really special finish, line the sides and base of the box with felt also.

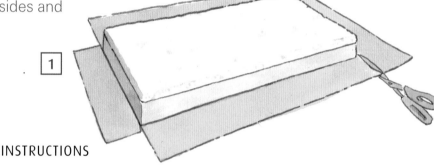

MATERIALS

- Checked shirts
- Felt to line the box
- Wadding
- Paper to make a pattern
- Fabric glue
- A shoe box

EQUIPMENT

- Dressmaking scissors
- Tape measure
- Pencil
- Paper-cutting scissors

INSTRUCTIONS

1 Cut the wadding to fit the top of the lid and glue it in place. Lay the lid on the paper and cut a pattern, adding twice the depth of the lid and wadding all around, plus 1¼ in (3 cm). Cut out the corners, with ½ in (1 cm) extra width on the flaps to cover the short sides.

2 Using the pattern as a guide, cut the fabric for the lid. Lay the lid with the wadding upside down on the wrong side of the fabric. Being careful not to distort the fabric, glue the long sides first to the underside of the lid. Repeat with the short sides, turning in the raw edges. Make a small cut at the corner to do this neatly.

3 Cut out a piece of felt to fit the inside of the lid. Glue in place, covering the raw edges. You can cover the base of the box in the same way. If you don't have a large enough piece of shirt, measure around all 4 sides and add 1¼ in (3 cm) as an overlap. Wrap the fabric around the box, turn the raw edges under, and glue in place. Turn the bottom and top edges under and glue in place.

TIP
You can add a pocket to one side of your box, as shown, simply by cutting a longer piece of fabric so you can create an overlap. Leave one end open so you can insert things in the side.

PLAID CLUTCH

There are some brightly colored plaids in both large and small scales. I chose two small-scale plaids to suit this small clutch. The size is ideal for carrying travel documents, keys, etc. The same design may be used to create larger or smaller bags. If you are making a larger bag, use a shirt with a bigger scale pattern, with a heavier interlining, and more substantial closure, perhaps a button and button hole.

MATERIALS

- 2 shirts in contrasting plaids
- Matching thread
- 20 in (50 cm) fusible interlining
- Press stud
- Paper to make a pattern

EQUIPMENT

- Pencil
- Pins
- Paper-cutting scissors
- Dressmaking scissors
- Sewing machine
- Needle

INSTRUCTIONS

1 Using the template on page 139, make a paper pattern for the flap. From each shirt and the interlining, cut out 1 flap. Make a second paper pattern 12½ x 9½ in (32 x 24 cm) for the bag section (this includes ½ in (1 cm) seam allowance). Cut 1 section from each shirt and the interlining (see pic. 1).

2

4 On the back of the bag, measure ⅝ in (1.5 cm) down from the top edge, then pin, baste, and machine stitch the flap onto the back of the bag. Fold the flap over to the front and mark its center point near the tip on the wrong side and sew on one half of the press stud. Sew the other half of the press stud on the bag front to correspond (see pic. 4).

2 Iron the interlining onto the wrong side of the flap and bag pieces cut from the outer fabric. Sandwich the interlining between the flap's outer and inner fabrics, with wrong sides together. On the flap, turn the curved edges under so that all the raw edges are hidden. Use a ¼ in (6 mm) seam allowance on the curved edges and a ½ in (1 cm) seam allowance along the top edge (see pic. 2). Pin, baste, and machine stitch around all edges.

3 With right sides facing out, sandwich the interlining between the bag inner piece and outer piece. Turn under the top and bottom edges by ½ in (1 cm) and pin, baste, and machine stitch the outer to the inner bag. Fold the bag in half so the outer fabric is facing inward, pin, baste, and machine stitch up the sides of the bag and then turn right side out.

4

APPLIQUÉD BOAT PILLOW

This kind of simple appliqué work has a naïve charm. It is quick and easy to do and because the stitching is so straightforward, this pillow makes an ideal first embellishment project for an inexperienced seamstress. A slightly sun-bleached linen shirt makes a great pillow for a bathroom chair. The boat motif is an easy one to follow and a good way to use up tiny pieces of leftover shirt fabric. The shirt placket makes a perfect, if somewhat fat, mast and the shirt buttons become portholes when sewn on the hull.

INSTRUCTIONS

1 From the large pale blue linen shirt, cut out the following: pillow front 18 x 18 in (46 x 46 cm), and two back pieces, each 12 x 18 in (30 x 46 cm). Put these to the side. Iron the fusible webbing onto the back of your fabric remnants and the shirt placket.

1

MATERIALS

- Large pale blue linen shirt
- Shirt remnants in assorted checks and stripes
- Shirt placket in royal blue
- Matching thread
- 20 in (50 cm) fusible webbing
- 4 white shirt buttons
- Pillow cushion, 14 x 14 in (36 x 36 cm)

EQUIPMENT

- Tape measure
- Pins
- Dressmaking scissors
- Iron and ironing board
- Pencil
- Needle
- Sewing machine

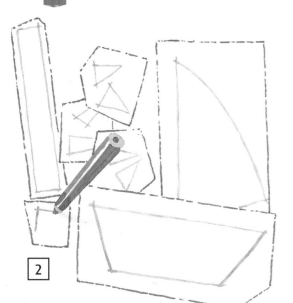

2

4 Using a loose running stitch, hand sew
around the edges of all the shapes. The
fusible webbing will hold them in place but
this stitching adds a decorative touch. Sew
the buttons along the center of the hull.

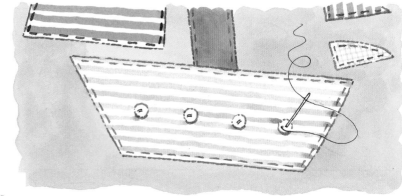

4

2 Remembering to draw in reverse, draw
a hull shape on the backing paper of one
of the striped pieces of fabric. Draw a large
sail in another striped fabric, and then six
triangles for the bunting on a selection of
the fabrics. Draw a small square shape to
go over the sail.

3

3 Cut out the shapes and carefully
remove the backing paper. Position them
in the center of the pillow front, on the
right side of the fabric and pin them in
place. When you are happy with their
position, iron them onto the pillow front.

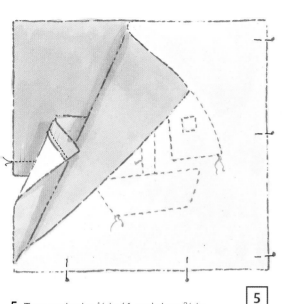

5 Turn under by ½ in (1 cm) then ¾ in (2 cm) one of the 18 in (46 cm) edges of the back piece of the pillow. Press, baste, and machine stitch. Repeat with the second back piece. Overlap the back pieces, with the neatened edges towards the center of the pillow, so that they are the same size as the pillow front piece. With right sides together, pin then baste the pillow front onto the two pillow backs. Machine stitch the front to the back of the pillow, ½ in (1 cm) from the edge. Turn right side out and press.

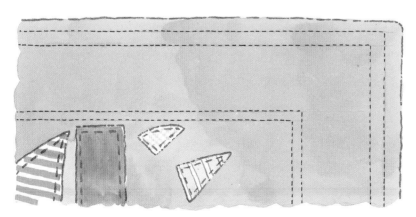

6 Using the sewing machine, top stitch ½ in (1 cm) in from the edge of the pillow cover on all four sides. Then add another line of top stitching ½ in (1 cm) in from the first line. Measure 2 in (5 cm) in from the last line of top stitching and add a third line. Add a fourth line ¼ in (6 mm) in from the one you have just stitched. This line will form the outline for the pillow cushion. Insert the pillow cushion through the opening at the back of the pillow.

SURFER DUDE'S FLOPPY HAT

If you have a sunny shirt, then why not make a hat for the sun? This one is reversible: I used a striped fabric for the inside and an abstract floral design for the outside. I had to make the brim from two sections to fit my shirts, but if you have large enough shirts you can make it in circular pieces, omitting the seam allowance.

MATERIALS

- 2 patterned shirts
- 20 in (50 cm) fusible interlining
- Matching thread
- Paper to make patterns

EQUIPMENT

- Pencil
- Pins
- Paper-cutting scissors
- Dressmaking scissors
- Sewing machine
- Needle

1

INSTRUCTIONS

1 Using the patterns on pages 138–139, cut out 4 of the crown section in each color scheme (see pic. 1). Cut out 2 of the rim in each color scheme. Cut 2 of the rim in fusible webbing.

2

4 Insert the lining hat into the outer hat and turn the outer rim seams under by ½ in (1 cm). Pin, baste, and machine stitch with a top stitch, attaching the brim upper to the brim lining. Attach the exterior of the hat to the inner hat by machine stitching with a line of running stitches ¼ in (6 mm) from the inner edge of the brim (see pic. 4). Wear with pride.

4

2 With right sides together, and using a seam allowance of ½ in (1 cm), pin, baste, and machine stitch the hat sections together, to form a kind of skull cap, in both color schemes (see pic. 2).

3 Iron the fusible webbing onto the brim pieces cut from the first fabric. With right sides together, machine stitch the two front and back seams of the rim together to form a circle. Do the same with the brim sections in the second fabric. Pin, baste, and machine stitch the first skull cap onto the circle you have just made, matching the fabric, right sides together. Do the same with the skull cap and brim in the second fabric.

SPORTY MEN'S SHIRTS

Most of the shirts I have discussed in previous chapters are made from woven cloth. Sports shirts are different—they are usually made from knitted cloth as this gives the garment stretch. A sports shirt needs to be light enough not to encumber the wearer and loose enough so as not to impede movement; it also needs to be able to transfer sweat away from the skin. Modern fabrics such as spandex do this job well.

A polo shirt is a tee-shaped shirt with short sleeves, a collar, and usually a two- or three-buttoned placket and an optional pocket. Early polo players actually wore something completely different: long-sleeved shirts made from Oxford cotton. It was René Lacoste, the French seven-time Grand Slam tennis player, who designed the tennis shirt as we know it today. In 1927, he embroidered the crocodile emblem on the left breast of his shirts. The tennis shirt, polo, and golf shirt are basically the same design. The differences are subtle: a golf shirt placket typically has three or four buttons, so it extends lower than a typical polo shirt. This iconic piece of clothing, which started off as sportswear, is now routinely worn for non-sporting activities too. This has a huge amount to do with Ralph Lauren's use of it as a form of casual attire.

Rugby shirts, with their distinctive stripes, are another style of shirt that has crossed the sport–into–fashion boundary. Traditionally they were made from cotton with rubber buttons. They are now a combination of natural and synthetic fabrics.

Apart from traditional tennis whites, most sports shirts are brightly colored with a combination of stripes, motifs, and club insignias. These interesting elements have been incorporated into the headboard design (see pages 132–135). The elasticity of a knitted shirt has been put to good use in the wheat pig (see pages 128–131). The contrast of dark and light gray stripes with a red Welsh rugby shirt lining was used to create a fabric hamper (see pages 124–127).

DRAWSTRING HAMPER

This project is made in the same way as the bread basket (see pages 86–89), but to a larger scale and with the addition of rope handles. It was initially intended as a recycling basket, but it will work equally as well as a laundry hamper. I used a striped rugby shirt for the outside and a red one to line it. It has been stiffened with interlining to give it body and prevent the sides from collapsing, but it still retains a softness that works well in any room.

INSTRUCTIONS

1 Either use a pencil and compass or draw around a plate to draw a circle on the pattern paper to the size you want: I used a circle with a diameter of 12 in (30 cm). Cut the circle out and fold into quarters. Measure the circumference of the circle. The easiest way to do this is to measure a quarter of the circle and multiply by 4. Add ¾ in (2 cm) for seam allowance. This measurement is the width of the shirt fabric needed for the sides of the cylinder. Cut a paper pattern for the sides of the bucket based on this measurement. Pin the paper pattern to the shirt to make sure you have enough fabric. If you cannot get a long enough piece of fabric from your shirt, you will have to join the sides of the cylinder—if so don't forget to add the seam allowances. Cut out your fabric.

MATERIALS

- A striped rugby shirt
- A plain red shirt
- Paper to make a pattern
- Matching thread
- 2.2 yd (2 m) fusible interlining
- Eyelet kit with 14 mm eyelets
- 1 m (39 in) rope or cord with a ½ in (1 cm) diameter

EQUIPMENT

- Compass or a plate to draw around
- Pencil
- Tape measure
- Paper-cutting scissors
- Dressmaking scissors
- Sewing machine
- Iron and ironing board

2 Using the same pattern piece, cut a piece of interlining and iron it onto the wrong side of the striped rugby shirt. Pin the circle pattern onto another section of the striped rugby shirt and cut that out. Cut a piece of interlining and iron it to the circle. With right sides together, pin, baste, and machine stitch the two narrow sides of the rectangle together to form a tube. Press seams flat. With right sides facing out, pin the base circle to one end of this tube. Pin at regular intervals, with the pins positioned at right angles to the edge. Baste, then machine stitch, feeding the fabric carefully through the machine and guiding it around the curved edge. Cut notches at regular intervals into the seam allowance. Press flat.

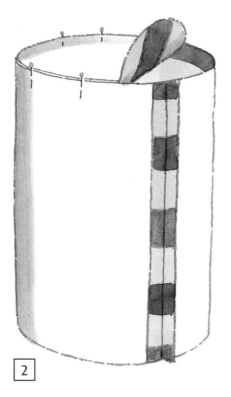

TIP
When fixing the base of the bin to the body of it you can reinforce it with an extra row of running stitches plus a zigzag stitch over the edges.

4 Following the manufacturer's instructions, punch holes to make eyelets at regular intervals 2 in (5 cm) from the top of the bucket. Finally, thread the rope through and tie with a reef knot.

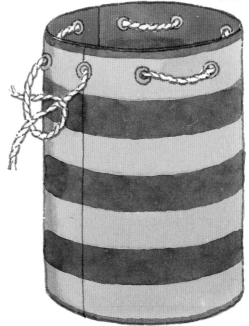

3 Repeat steps 1 and 2 with the red shirt fabric. Insert the red bucket into the striped bucket. Turn the raw top edges of both under ¾ in (2 cm) and then pin, baste, and machine stitch the inner to the outer bucket, with a line of top stitching.

DEEP HEAT PIGGY

Make this little piggy out of a knitted sports shirt fabric so that it has lots of give and stretch. Fill it with a mixture of wheat and lavender, place it in the microwave to heat up, and then just give it a hug. It is perfect for those suffering from back pain or simply wanting a warm cuddle. I chose a white sports shirt with a pink stripe. You could choose a yellow sports shirt to make a duck shape. Keep the shape simple and wide enough to fit your back.

MATERIALS

- A stretchy sports shirt
- Matching thread
- 2 bags of wheat (available from health food shops)
- 1 small bag of dried lavender (optional)
- Paper to make a pattern
- Black bead or button for the eye

EQUIPMENT

- Pencil
- Paper-cutting scissors
- Pins
- Dressmaking scissors
- Sewing machine
- Iron and ironing board
- Needle

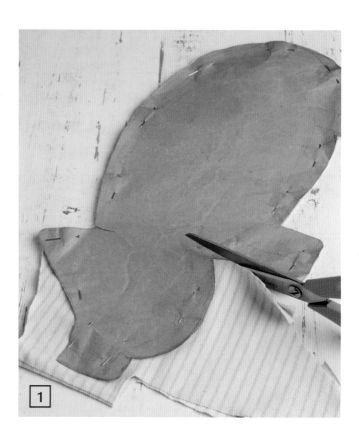

INSTRUCTIONS

1 Using the template on pages 140–141, make a paper pattern. Pin it onto two layers of the shirt material. Cut out 2 pieces, a front and a back (see pic. 1).

TIP

To use, heat in a microwave at
500 w for 2 minutes or 750 w
for 1 minute. If you need to wash
your wheat-filled animal, undo the
opening, remove the filling, and wash
for the fabric type. Refill with wheat,
close up the opening, and use again.

2 To make the tail, cut a strip of the shirt 9 x 1¾ in (23 x 4.5 cm). Fold this in half lengthwise and iron the crease. Turn the outside edges to the middle, so all the raw edges are hidden, and iron again. Pin, baste, and machine stitch down the length (see pic. 2).

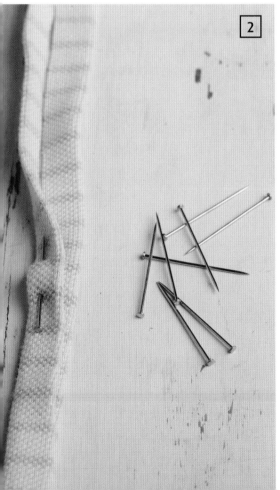

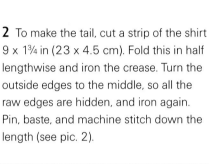

3 With right sides together, and the tail sandwiched between the front and back, pin, baste, and machine stitch around most of the pig, leaving a gap at the bottom to insert the wheat. Turn right side out, iron flat, then carefully fill the bag with the wheat and lavender—use a plastic funnel to make this easier. Close up the gap using slip stitch. Bend the ear down and catch with a stitch. Bend the tail around and around and then catch with a stitch so you have a curly tail. Finally, sew on a bead or button for the eye.

SPORTS FAN'S HEADBOARD

I decorated an old headboard using the fabric, motifs, and numbers from sports shirts. This is a fun project for a sports-crazy child and you can really personalize it by using their own old sports shirts that they have outgrown. You can even include the name of their team or logos of teams they support.

MATERIALS

- Old sports shirts in different colors
- Matching thread
- An old fabric-covered, padded headboard
- Fusible webbing

EQUIPMENT

- Staple remover or pliers
- Dressmaking scissors
- Pins
- Sewing machine
- Iron and ironing board
- Tailors' chalk
- Needle
- Staple gun and staples

1 Using the staple remover or pliers, carefully remove the old cover from the headboard. Retain the fabric cut from the headboard to use as a pattern for your new cover. Cut the sports shirts into large rectangular shapes, being careful to put aside for later use any interesting motifs, such as stripes and numbers. Arrange the pieces into a pleasing composition.

2 With right sides together, pin one shape onto the next and baste and machine stitch using a ½ in (1 cm) seam allowance. Press the seams flat. Lay this patchwork wrong side up, then lay the old headboard cover on top, wrong side up. Draw around it with tailors' chalk and then cut your shape.

3 Iron the numbers and shapes you cut from the shirts onto fusible webbing, and then carefully cut them out. Arrange them on your patchwork of shapes. When you are happy with the design, peel away the backing paper and iron the motifs onto the cover. Machine stitch around the edges of each shape to secure them to the headboard cover.

4 Pin the patchwork of shirts onto the headboard. Stretching the fabric, and folding neatly at the corners, start at the center of the top edge on the back of the headboard and work outwards, stapling the cover onto the headboard. Start again from the center, stapling outward to the other side. Repeat this process on the bottom edge, working from the center as before. Then do the two short sides in the same way.

TEMPLATES

Trace using these shapes, or xerox them. Use as actual size unless otherwise indicated—if you need or wish to enlarge any, use a xerox machine. To make your patterns, use strong paper such as Kraft paper. Always cut out paper with paper-cutting scissors or you will blunt your dressmaking scissors.

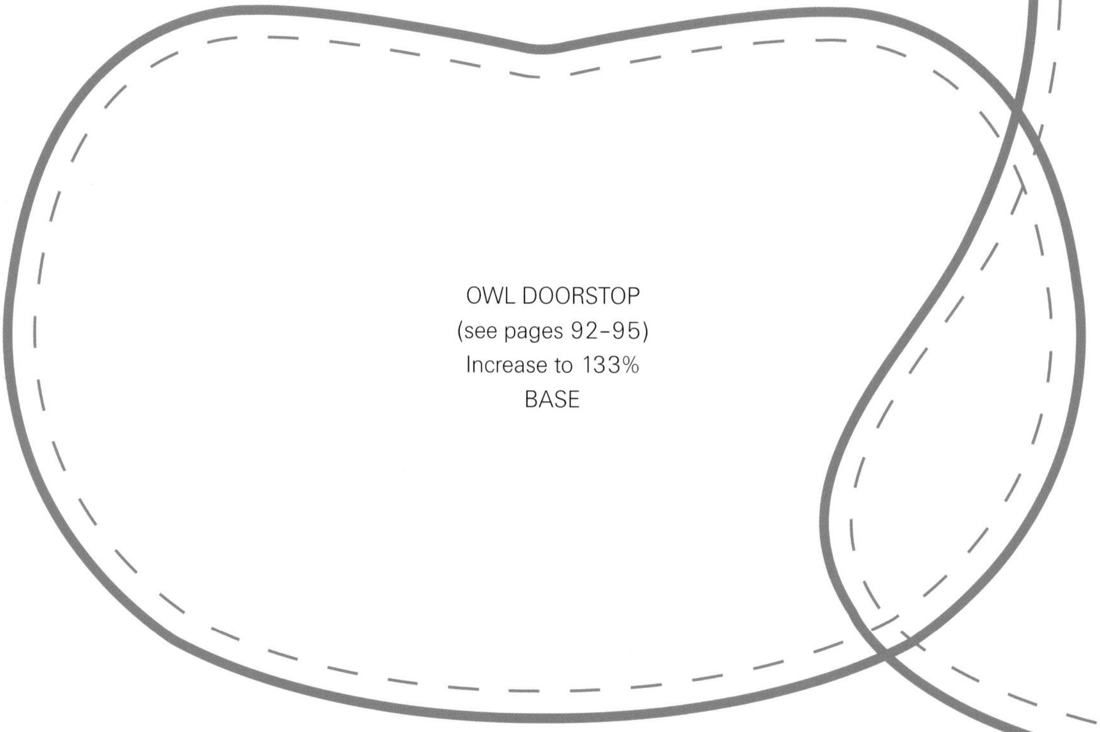

OWL DOORSTOP
(see pages 92–95)
Increase to 133%
BASE

OWL DOORSTOP
(see pages 92–95)
Increase to 133%
BODY

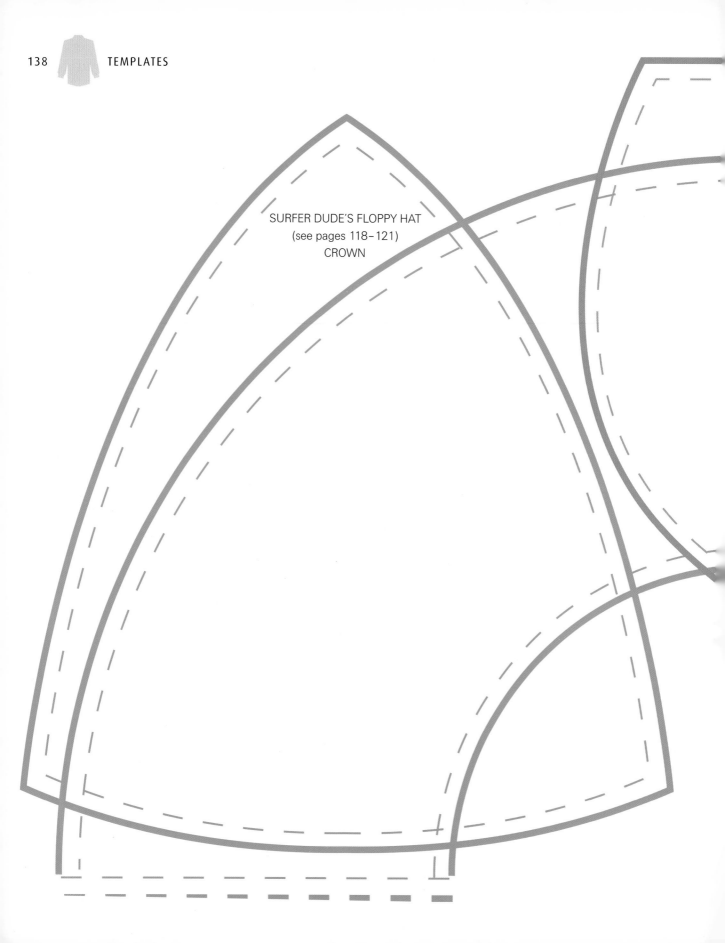

SURFER DUDE'S FLOPPY HAT
(see pages 118–121)
CROWN

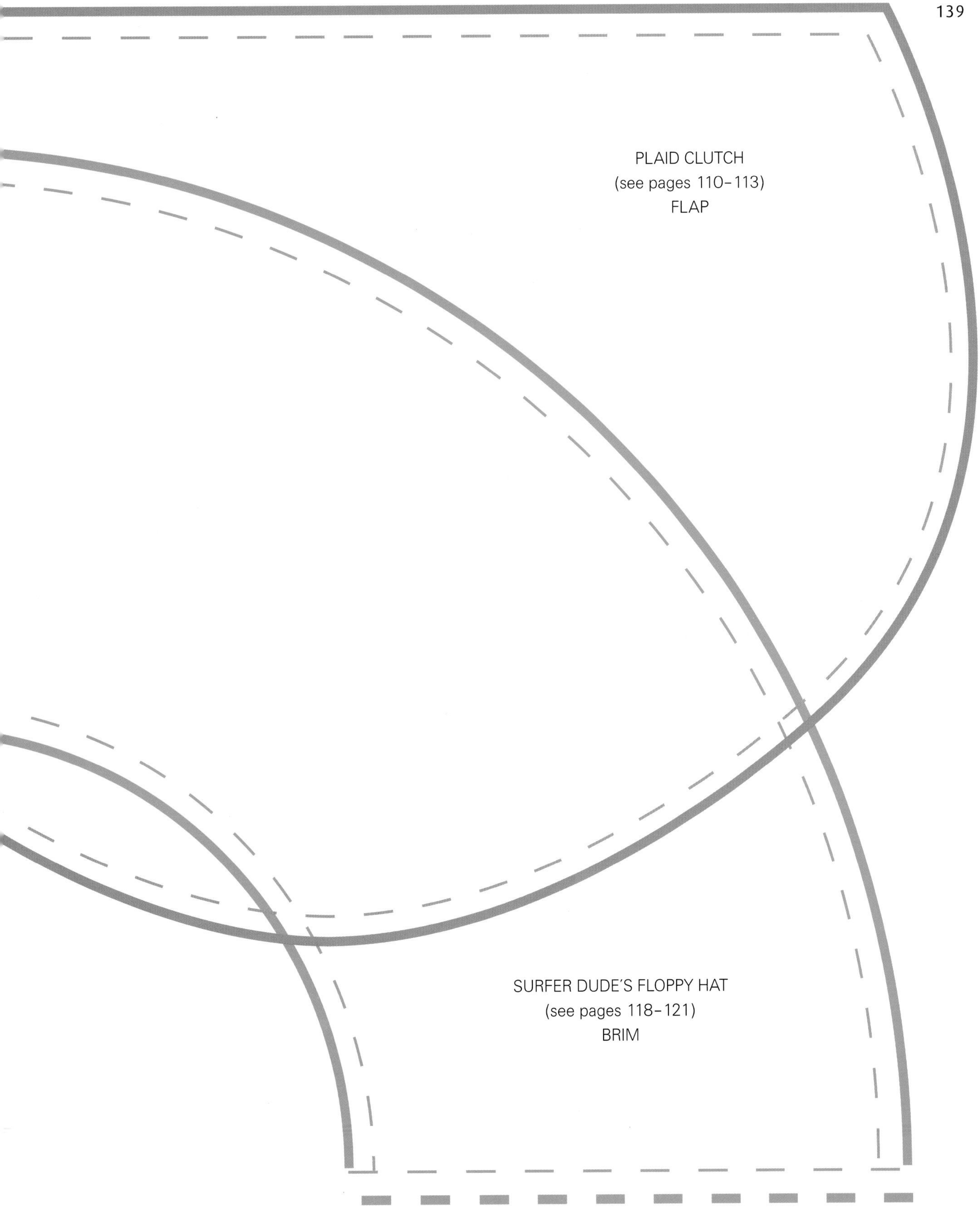

PLAID CLUTCH
(see pages 110–113)
FLAP

SURFER DUDE'S FLOPPY HAT
(see pages 118–121)
BRIM

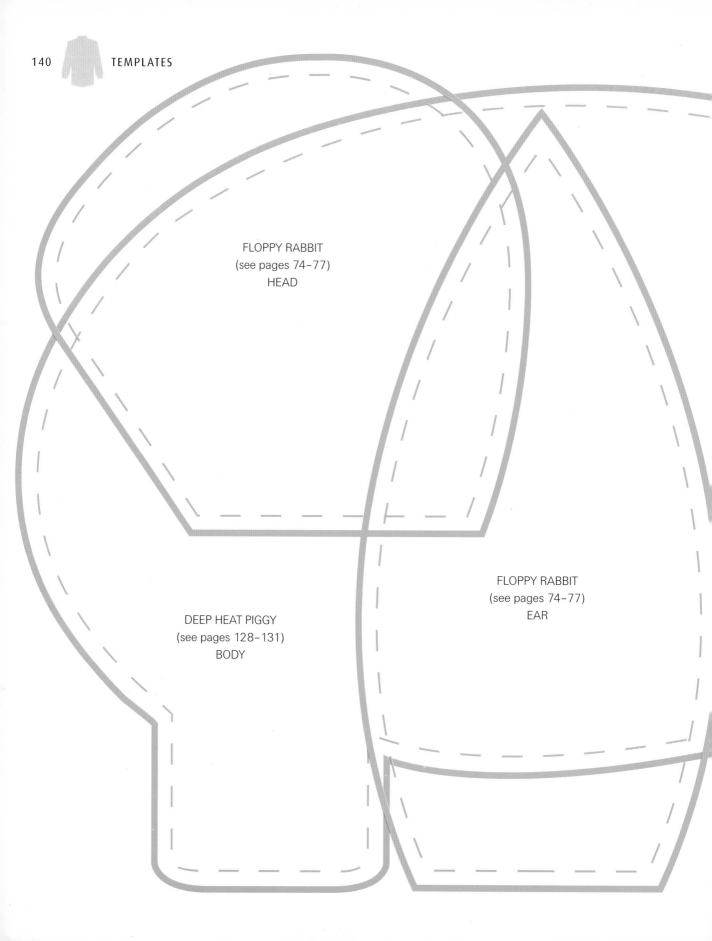

FLOPPY RABBIT
(see pages 74–77)
HEAD

FLOPPY RABBIT
(see pages 74–77)
EAR

DEEP HEAT PIGGY
(see pages 128–131)
BODY

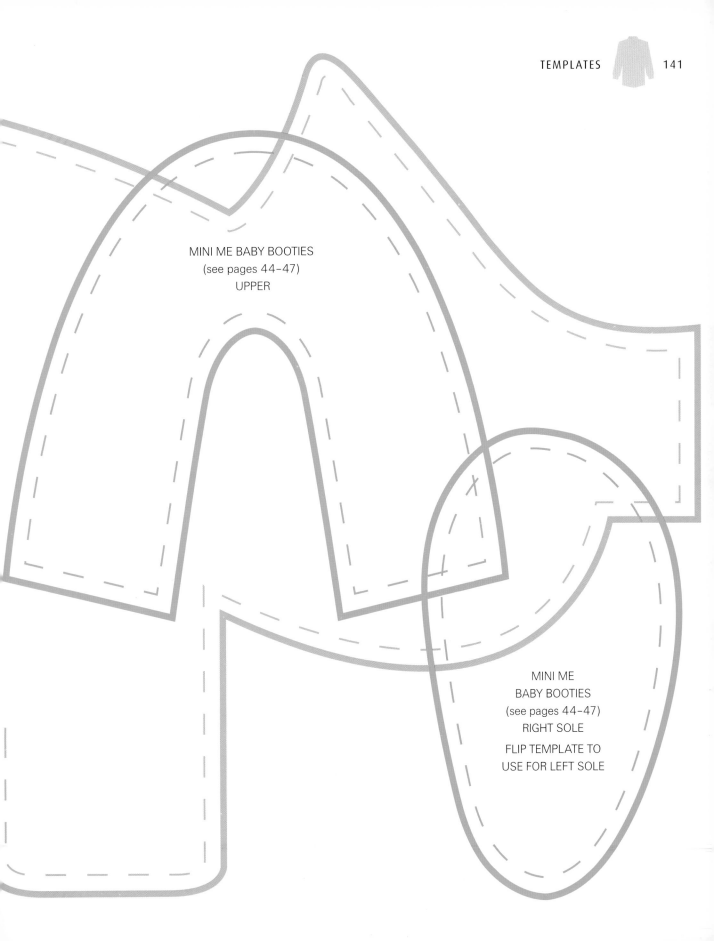

MINI ME BABY BOOTIES
(see pages 44–47)
UPPER

MINI ME
BABY BOOTIES
(see pages 44–47)
RIGHT SOLE

FLIP TEMPLATE TO
USE FOR LEFT SOLE

DIRECTORY

WHERE TO FIND SHIRTS

If you are going to make any of the projects in this book you are going to need shirts. I am tempted to say beg, borrow, or steal, but please don't do the last of these. It is not kind to the significant other in your life to cut up his shirts without first getting his permission to do so.

After I had started writing this book I attended the Festival of Quilts at the National Exhibition Centre in Birmingham, England, where I stumbled upon a delightful, exquisitely fashioned quilt made from pieced shirts called "Where have all my shirts gone?" I rest my case. I loved the quilt so much, I bought it from the makers Joan Herrington and Rosalind Gregory.

FRIENDS

Ask friends, colleagues, and friends of friends to remember you when they are throwing out old or no longer wanted shirts. It doesn't matter if they are frayed at the cuffs or stained under the arms—all these parts can be cut away and the rest of the shirt put to good use.

CHARITY SHOPS

Visit charity or thrift shops and ask if you can buy a bag of the old shirts they would otherwise sell for recycling as rags. The other alternative is to buy at the price the charity shop wishes to sell at, and you can come away with a shirt and a warm glow, knowing you have helped someone.

THINK CREATIVELY

I wanted to make something out of a corduroy shirt, but most of them were in drab colors, so I dyed one a bright green. Machine dyes are so easy to use and the result can be quite stunning. Dye sellers can be found on the Internet: *www.ritdye.com*.

SHIRTMAKERS

These are some of my favorite shirtmakers, and are ones to look for when sourcing second-hand shirts. If you spot them, snap them up!

Ben Sherman
www.brand.bensherman.com

Boden
www.bodenusa.com

Calvin Klein
www.calvinkleininc.com

Charles Tyrwhitt
www.ctshirts.com

Fat Face
www.fatface.com

Gap
www.gap.com

Hackett London
www.hackett.com

Jack Wills
www.jackwills.com

Joules
www.joules.com

Old Navy
www.oldnavy.gap.com

Pink
www.thomaspink.com

Prowse & Hargood
www.prowseandhargood.com

Ralph Lauren
www.ralphlauren.com

Ted Baker
www.tedbaker.com/men's/shirts

White Stuff
www.whitestuff.com

CRAFT SUPPLIERS

In addition to shirts, you will need sewing items: webbing, threads, scissors, needles, etc.

Michaels Stores
1-800-642-4235
www.michaels.com

JoAnn Fabric and Craft Stores
1-888-739-4120
www.joann.com

AC Moore
1-888-ACMOORE
www.acmoore.com

Save on Crafts
831-768-8428
www.save-on-crafts.com

eNasco
1-800-558-9595
www.enasco.com

Sewing and Craft Superstore
www.craftysewer.com
This is where I purchased the fabric stiffener for blinds that I used on the lamp and shade (see pages 48–51).

S&S Worldwide
1-800-288-9941
www.ssww.com

ACKNOWLEDGMENTS

Thank you to the following people for their help and encouragement while this book was being written:

The publisher
First and foremost to Jacqui Small for going with the idea. Despite a volcano in Iceland and lack of foreign buyers at The London Book Fair and Frankfurt, she stuck with it.

The shirt finders and providers
Shiva Pius from All Aboard'charity shop in Streatham.
Linda Hudgins from the Cancer Research shop in Putney.
Dr. Cosmo Hallstrom for donating a very splendid lumberjack shirt.
The Trinity Hospice, Fara, Cancer Reseach shops in Balham.
Age U.K. in Clapham.

The young people who modeled
Barney Eliot and Matt Skidmore who modeled the apron, stripping off manfully to try on prototypes while I honed the design.
Jay Howarth and Rosa Roberts who modeled the finished apron for the book.

The makers
A very big thank you to Aniko Szabo for sewing the following projects: baby booties, wheat pig, garden chair covers, dining chair cover, bunting, cafetière cover, floppy hat, and drawstring hamper.
Callie Anderson for making the gorgeous bunny.
Barney Eliot for covering the boxes.

The product suppliers
Thanks to Dylon for giving me machine dye that enabled me to transform a rather shabby-looking corduroy shirt into a gorgeous fern green color.
Nick Bevan from Homecrafts Direct for supplying me with craft materials.

The book producers
Caroline Arber for her gorgeous, miraculous summer photographs taken in gloomy January.
Maggie Town for overseeing the shoots and being so encouraging.
Sian Parkhouse for editing, Kate Simunek for her lovely illustrations, and Kerenza Swift and Jo Copestick for being at the other end of the phone.

The family
My surprisingly forbearing husband who lost his "frostbite series" spinnaker trimmer, and my children who had to just see less of me.